Supratim Sarkar, a 1997 batch officer of the Indian Police Service, is presently Additional Commissioner of Police, Kolkata. A voracious reader and an erstwhile journalist, his passions include cricket and ancient history. He is an alumnus of Presidency College, Kolkata. He lives in Kolkata with his wife and two children.

Swati Sengupta is an author and journalist based in Kolkata. Her published books are *Out of War* (Speaking Tiger, 2016), *Half the Field Is Mine* (Scholastic, 2014), *Guns on My Red Earth* (Red Turtle, Rupa, 2013) and *The Talking Bird* (Tulika Books, 2014). Swati studied English at Jadavpur University and then worked as a journalist for fourteen years for various newspapers in Kolkata. She runs a workshop on gender for the young called *Elephant in the Room* and spearheaded the much talked about Dear Boys project in Kolkata schools supported by the Kolkata Police, in which she addressed gender issues with teenage boys. She loves small towns, tea and the chirping of birds, and lives in a brave and beautiful world in which girls and boys do not carry out gender-specific roles.

MURDER IN THE CITY

TWELVE INCREDIBLE CASE FILES OF THE KOLKATA POLICE

Supratim Sarkar

Translated by Swati Sengupta

SPEAKING TIGER

SPEAKING TIGER PUBLISHING PVT. LTD
4381/4, Ansari Road, Daryaganj,
New Delhi–110002, India

First published in paperback by Speaking Tiger 2018

ISBN: 978-93-87693-00-5
eISBN: 978-93-87164-83-3

10 9 8 7 6 5 4 3 2 1

Typeset in Minion Pro by SÜRYA, New Delhi
Printed at

CONTENTS

FOREWORD

Writing a foreword for a book written by Supratim Sarkar who has been eulogized in cyberspace as the best thing to happen to Bengali detective story writing in recent times, put me under a lot of pressure. I searched for tips on the Internet and found that if you have been asked to write a foreword, it means that you are already a published writer or have accomplished something in life. I realized that none of these holds true for me. I have no books to my name and I have been asked to write the foreword because I head one of most distinguished police forces in the country. And then suddenly, I noted that of all the books written by brilliant writers which I have read, I don't remember even one name of the person who wrote the foreword or the contents of that foreword. That was quite a liberating thought and instantly the pressure vanished.

In fact, the 'storm' that the stories in this book created, when they were put on the Kolkata Police Facebook page and Kolkata Police website, literally forced us to bring these out in a book form. The reaction about the writing style was truly overwhelming. And let truth be told, it is difficult to leave a story in the middle once you have started reading it. It is no mean achievement considering the fact that the writer did not have even the slightest liberty of playing with the facts and basic line of investigation. Here before you is the English translation of these stories done by Swati Sengupta, an author in her own right, which I am sure readers will like as much as they have enjoyed reading the original Bengali version.

This book is not only about good storytelling but also about the real-life flavour of these stories. The cases solved in these stories are not a figment of the imagination of the writer but indicative of the hard work and skill of Kolkata Police detectives. You will not find a 'Sherlock Homes' or a 'Hercule Poirot' solving cases but each case shows the detective skills of the Kolkata Police officers—skills that match the best in the world.

It is a real honour and privilege to head a force which has brilliant detectives like the ones showcased in this book and also outstanding writers like Supratim Sarkar. The professionalism of Kolkata Police officers did not surprise me one bit, but I must confess, Supratim's writing style came across as a pleasant surprise. Great writing combined with brilliant detective skills make this book an instant winner.

In the best traditions of detective storytelling, I would like to draw the attention of readers to an unsolved murder case which happened exactly sixty-nine years ago in another continent. On 1 Dec 1948, in Australia, a body of an unidentified Caucasian male was found with no identification marks on his person whatsoever except a piece of paper torn off the famous Omar Khayyam book *Rubiayat*, on which was written 'Tamam Shud' (it is a Persian phrase meaning 'finished' or 'ended'). Readers must be familiar with 'kaam tamam' (frequently used in Hindi) to indicate 'murder', which has the same Persian root. Investigators found that someone had done a professional job of removing all possible identification marks from the clothes of the deceased. This case has been called Australia's most baffling murder mystery and still remains unsolved despite considerable interest and effort undertaken by the Australian Police and even the academic world. It is widely believed that the man was killed by an undetectable poison. That particular edition of *Rubiayat* was located during the investigation and investigators found an encrypted message written in that book, which to date has not been decrypted. Readers interested in exercising their mental faculties may like to have a crack at this code which investigators believe might lead to the actual identity of the murderer.

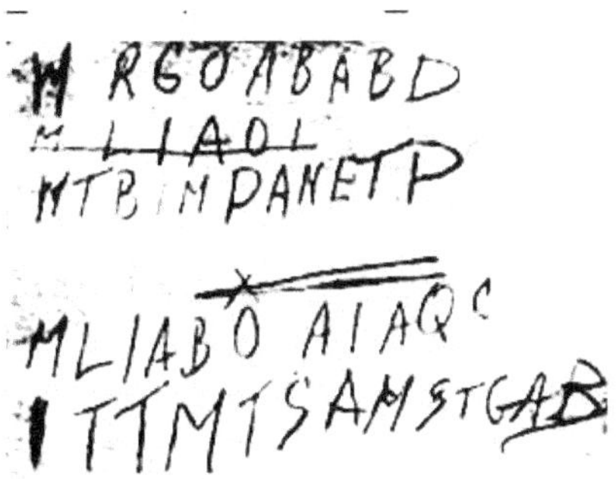

Wish all readers a happy and enjoyable reading.

Rajeev Kumar, IPS
Commissioner of Police, Kolkata
December 2017

THORN IN THE FLESH

The Amarendra Pandey murder case (also known as the Pakur murder case), 1934

Tollygunge police station. Case number 67. Date: 17 February 1934. Indian Penal Code Sections 302 and 120B: murder and criminal conspiracy.

'Uff! What on earth did he pierce into my arm?'

A sudden stabbing sensation made the twenty-year-old man pull up the sleeves of his kurta and examine his upper arm. It looked like a simple pinprick but he had begun to feel a dreadful burning sensation already...

26 November 1933. An ordinary afternoon was quickly taking strides towards evening time, as if it were rushed off its feet. A sea of people had crammed Howrah station—coolies carrying oversized bulky baggage were calling out their urgent, peremptory *thoda side dijiye bhaisaab* (brother, please give me some space). Trains were chugging in and out of the station, smoke billowing from them, and announcements of their arrival and departure were being made over the loudspeaker.

A small group on the railway platform was drawing the attention of passersby. Amarendra Chandra Pandey—youngest scion of the Pakur zamindari was going home and something akin to a grand send-off was occurring at the station. Amarendra and his sister Bonobala were setting off for Pakur (in neighbouring Bihar then, now in

Jharkhand) and their close friends Kamalaprasad Pandey, Ashok Prakash Mitra and several others were standing around them. Their step-brother, Vinayendra, had also come to the farewell congregation, though he did not actually *belong* there. He was more of an interloper, a thorn in their flesh.

The train was about to leave any moment, but the farewells were not over yet. Suddenly, a man wrapped in a grimy shawl came from the opposite direction, darted towards Amarendra, and after slightly nudging him, melted into the crowd. The very next moment, Amarendra felt a sharp jab of pain—'Uff! What on earth did he pierce into my arm?'

The Amarendra Pandey murder case (also known as the Pakur murder case) was investigated by the Kolkata Police more than eighty-five years ago. It is deemed to be one of the most puzzling cases in the list of extraordinary probes conducted by the country's oldest Commissionerate. It is still mentioned in discussions on crime and police investigation researches as 'one of the first cases of individual bioterrorism in modern world history'.

Details of this case are widely available on the Internet, yet confusion prevails due to a lack of authenticity of the sources. This narrative has been taken from the Kolkata Police case diary—well preserved in the Kolkata Police Museum on Archarya Prafulla Chandra Road—on display for visitors.

Pakur district is now one of the twenty-four districts of Jharkhand. It used to be a sub-division of Santhal Pargana district since 1868 (it became a separate district only in 1994). Famous for its black stone, Pakur was an administrative centre of the district for many years. To the north lies Sahibgunj, Dumka to the south, Godda in the west and West Bengal's Murshidabad and Birbhum districts to its east.

Pakur's Pandey family was one of the richest zamindars during pre-Independence days.

Zamindar Pratapendra Chandra Pandey had married twice—Vinayendra and Kananbala were his children from the first marriage, and Amarendra and Bonobala from the second marriage. Pratapendra's elder brother had died young, leaving behind his widow, Suryavati Devi. The couple had no children.

When the events described here occurred, Pratapendra's wives had both passed away. In fact, Amarendra's mother had died just a few weeks after his birth, and Suryavati Devi, his aunt, who had no children, had brought up Amarendra as her own child. He was the apple of her eyes, close to her heart, whom she had coddled and cosseted all through his childhood and beyond.

Pratapendra and Suryavati Devi had divided the property equally, and there had been no dispute or discontent on any front over it. The annual earning from the property crossed rupees one lakh—the amount itself indicative of the family's prosperity.

Pratapendra died in 1929 bequeathing his share of the property equally between his two sons Vinayendra and Amarendra. There was only one technical problem—Amarendra, who was younger, was fifteen years old at the time, a minor and still a school-going child. Therefore his half-brother Vinayendra, then a young man of twenty-two years, was entrusted with Amarendra's share till he became an adult. He was expected to hand it over when his brother turned eighteen.

Vinayendra led a dissolute life, excessively fond of drinking and women. These two were the driving forces in his life. He frequently visited two women of apparent ill-repute—Balikabala and Chanchala. Sometimes he would travel to distant Mumbai (then Bombay), drawn by the allure of the film industry's glitz and glamour. Naturally, he was averse to regimen, restraint or control, and had been so right from his teenage days.

Amarendra belonged to the other side of the spectrum—gentlemanly, upholder of high ethical and moral standards, keen on pursuing a higher education, with a penchant for a regular fitness regime. These qualities naturally made him popular among the people of Pakur, all of whom loved their Chhotobabu, the younger of the scions, to bits.

After passing out of school, Amarendra joined Patna College. Vinayendra—not unexpectedly—often delayed sending his brother's fees and money for other expenses. In 1932, when he was in the fourth year of college, Amarendra turned eighteen. The teenager was mature for his years and, knowing his brother's nature, did not think it would be prudent to delay seeking the rightful possession of his share of the property. Accordingly, he shot off a letter to Vinayendra.

Suryavati Devi had also advised him to do this. She lived in Deoghar, which is about 150 km from Pakur, and she was in regular touch with Amarendra. Completely aware of Vinayendra's vicious waywardness, she advised the younger brother to demand his share right away.

Vinayendra, naturally, was loath to losing a large part of the property to his step-brother. It would leave him with less money to fritter away. But the law was not on his side, as his father's will was iron clad, and despite the reluctance, he had to hand over a share equivalent to his own portion to his brother. This entire episode was fraught with acerbic conversations, unpleasant exchange of letters, and bitterness between the two brothers.

During Durga Puja that year, Amarendra visited Suryavati in Deoghar. To their surprise, Vinayendra, too, visited there after a few days—almost as if he were tailing Amarendra. The awkwardness between the two brothers compelled Vinayendra to rent temporary accommodation for himself.

One evening, Vinayendra dropped by and proposed that the two of them go on a short walk. 'Babu, come let's go on a stroll,' he told his brother with great enthusiasm. Babu was Amarendra's pet name. He agreed, despite all the bitterness and resentment.

The two were out for a while that evening. Amarendra traipsed around with Vinanyendra hoping it would be over soon. Suddenly, taking him completely by surprise, Vinayendra fished out something from his pocket. It closely resembled a pair of spectacles. 'Look what I got for you from Kolkata!' He was holding a pair of pince-nez glasses in his hands. He insisted that Amarendra wear the glasses—a stylish and luxurious possession those days. Despite Amarendra's mild objections, Vinayendra had his way. In fact, he ended up almost jamming the spectacles on Amarendra's nose.

The mild resistance ended up hurting Amarendra's nose, but he was too taken aback by his brother's odd behaviour to react immediately. He found that the glasses had even cut his nose a bit.

Did Vinayendra put a wee bit more pressure than was required? Amarendra was not sure, and he confided to his friends and Suryavati about it. But it was, after all, a tiny bruise, so it remained a mere suspicion, not a presentiment of disaster—as a disaster is what it eventually turned out to be. After three days, his face swelled up massively, numbing all senses around the nose. The family physician was called in and he diagnosed it as an attack of tetanus. Amarendra was immediately given the anti-tetanus injection.

By then, Vinayendra had returned to Kolkata. In fact, he had gone back immediately after the attack on his brother. But that did not stop him from making sure that his attack was successful.

Accordingly, he sent a young doctor from Kolkata for Amarendra's treatment. The doctor, Taranath Bhattacharya, had a way with people—a great gift of the gab, something that instantly captivated others. But somehow, despite his best efforts, Bhattacharya was not successful. He proposed the use of morphine for quick recovery, but the doctors who had kept Amarendra under round-the-clock supervision, promptly shot down the idea.

Next, Vinayendra himself landed up in Deoghar, accompanied by an apparently even more experienced physician, Dr Durgaratan Dhar. This doctor was perhaps more persuasive, for he gave Amarendra an injection that he had carried all the way from Kolkata. Soon after injecting the medicine, Dr Dhar and Vinayendra left Deoghar under the pretext of a medical emergency that required the doctor's urgent attention.

Within an hour of the injection, Amarendra's condition began to deteriorate. He began to flit precariously between consciousness and semiconsciousness, and his blood pressure started fluctuating. But somehow, he managed to pull through. It was a close shave that time.

Vinayendra was back in Deoghar soon—this time along with the same Dr Dhar and another new entrant, Dr Shibapada Bhattacharya. But by then, Amarendra's relatives and other well wishers were too infuriated to allow his step-brother anywhere close to him. Suryavati had given strict instructions to not allow Vinayendra anywhere in Amarendra's vicinity. After several futile attempts and many arguments with her, Vinayendra had to swallow his pride and returned to Kolkata with his line-up of doctors.

Suryavati however, was now really worried about her beloved Amarendra. His health was a constant worry for her. The boy who used to wake up at five in the morning and exercise regularly, was now unable to leave his bed before 10 a.m. due to a debilitating weakness. His condition did not improve even after a year.

In 1933, Amarendra was taken to Kolkata in the hope that better medical care might help him bounce back to life. A house on Harish Mukherjee Road was taken on rent. The doctor on call was the celebrated Nil Ratan Sircar (the N.R.S. Medical College & Hospital in Kolkata is named after him). Dr Sarkar prescribed medicines and advised a break from his work schedule along with a trip outside the city to get clean, fresh air and ample rest.

Following this advice, Amarendra went on a vacation to Bhubaneswar, in adjoining Odisha. But there wasn't much improvement—he continued to be struck by the same crippling fatigue that restricted him to bed for large parts of the day, he was dizzy at times, and had poor appetite. Once a voracious reader who enjoyed the company of books, he now turned away from reading much to the surpise of everyone around him. His friends brought an endless supply of books for him, but Amarendra would leaf through a few pages and then put them aside. After a few months, he returned to Pakur and got back to work, albeit in frail health.

All the while the sprightly Amarendra was turning into a weak, diseased man, Vinayendra was hard at work. He was planning meticulously how to deal the final blow.

18 November 1933. Amarendra received a telegram from Suryavati Devi which read—'Property levy-related legal matters. Rush to Kolkata.' Amarendra urgently reached Kolkata only to discover that it was a bogus telegram—Suryavati was neither in Kolkata nor had she sent any such telegram.

When Amarendra informed her about the trick, she was filled with dread. It was no mystery, nor did it take a great deal of effort to guess who had sent the hoax letter. Only, it was impossible to predict what Vinayendra's next trap would be.

'Don't let Dada come anywhere close to you,' Suryavati pleaded. When Amarendra asked his brother about the telegram, he turned combative and denied everything with a dramatic shrug.

All this while, Vinayendra also made several failed attempts at forging Amarendra's signature in order to withdraw a lion's share from their joint account deposit of two lakh rupees. It was no small amount, and when Amarendra learnt about this from their family lawyer, it led to bitter altercations between the brothers all over again.

25 November 1933. Amarendra was due to leave for Pakur from Kolkata the next day. That evening, Vinayendra made a sudden appearance in the house rented by Amarendra.

Playing the role of a repentant man who deeply cared about his younger brother, Vinayendra muttered with a sheepish grin, 'Don't misunderstand me, Babu. Take care of your health'. His voice choked and he referred to many childhood memories in his conversation. Amarendra was well versed with his brother's crafty ways and wasn't the least moved by these acts. But unknown to him, the real purpose behind Vinayendra's visit had been served—he had tricked his younger brother into disclosing the departure time of his train the following day.

Next day: November 26.

At the station, Amarendra's family members and friends were astonished to find Vinayendra hanging around there again. 'What is this scum doing here?' some of them asked. Amarendra allayed their fears. What if he was there, Amarendra said to them. He was a brother, after all. Amarendra had absolutely no idea what was coming his way. A few moments later, a man wrapped in a dirty shawl sprang out from the crowd, pricked him with a needle-like object and vanished into the crowds before anyone realized what had happened.

Amarendra checked the wound. It looked negligible. A colourless liquid was seeping out from where the needle or pin had perforated the flesh. A few drops of this liquid had stained the sleeve of his kurta. There were still five minutes left for the train's departure. His sister Bonobala was sick with panic, as were Kamalaprasad and the other friends. Let's cancel the journey they said, and suggested Amarendra visit a doctor right away. Vinayendra, too, pretended to be greatly concerned, but made a quick and subtle change of stance: 'You can visit a doctor on reaching Pakur, can't you?' When Kamalaprasad insisted that a visit to the doctor was urgent, Vinayendra pretended to lose his cool and bragged, 'We are scions of the Pakur zamindari. We aren't worried about silly things like ordinary people.'

Finally Amarendra decided to leave for Pakur as planned as he had some important work to attend to after a couple of days. A change of travel plans could jeopardise matters, he thought, and a doctor could address the wound once he reached home. So he boarded the train—an act that would prove fatal.

Bonobala continued to worry throughout the journey. 'Dadabhai, I am so worried,' she told Amarendra over and over again during their train journey.

'About what?'

'I can't forget the way the man injured your arm.'

'I don't think it is something to be worried about. Maybe he was a pickpocket trying to steal some money. Maybe he had a knife on him.'

'Would a knife make such a perforation? Doesn't it look rather odd? I am beginning to think I may have seen the man somewhere... but I just cannot recall where...'

'What are you saying! You are imagining things now.'

'I don't think so. I am sure now that I have seen him somewhere. Such uncanny similarity...'

'I saw him quite clearly at the station. He was short, dark with a grimy shawl wrapped around himself, wearing slippers.'

'Dadabhai! Yes, I clearly recall now! Remember we went to Purna cinema hall to watch a movie last week? That man was walking aimlessly around the ticket counter.'

'I am sure you are mistaken. How can you remember every vagabond in the city? Don't worry about it.'

But Bonobala's worst fears came true. Amarendra fell

seriously ill in some hours, and the following day was rushed to Kolkata. The family rented a house on Rash Behari Avenue. This time, another reputed physician, Dr Nalini Ranjan Sengupta, was called.

Dr Sengupta prescribed a detailed 'blood culture' immediately. Amarendra's whole arm had swollen up, his temperature was stuck at 105 degrees, his pressure and heartbeat were shooting up and coming down rapidly—the overall condition was quickly deteriorating. It was going beyond the doctors' control.

On December 3, Amarendra sank into a coma, and died the following day. The blood culture report came the day after his death, leaving the doctors in silent terror and disbelief. There was *Pasteurella Pestis* bacteria in the blood—the plague bacteria. There was no doubt now that Amarendra had died of the plague.

Since it was an apparently natural death, there was no need for a post mortem, and the body was cremated. Social and family rules required elder brother Vinayendra to do the main rituals at the cremation. Through it all,Vinayendra never stopped sobbing for a moment, never giving a hint of his role in the despicable act that had been committed.

Though there was no post mortem, Amarendra's friends and family members had no doubt about Vinayendra's hand in Amarendra's death, and were treating it as murder. But where was the proof? It was absurd to want to punish someone in the absence of evidence, no matter how strong or convincing the suspicion.

The unusual death had a serious impact elsewhere, too. It set some renowned doctors of Kolkata thinking how a healthy young man, used to a regular fitness regime could suddenly die of plague! They spoke with his friends and relatives, and took relevant notes including the pin pricking episode at the railway station. They took it upon themselves to solve the riddle that could not be explained by logic and years of experience. It was a professional affront after all, a wavering of the firm base of the towering positions they had come to occupy in their area of work.

Accordingly, they sent a letter to the Director of Tropical Medicine on February 12. Was it possible to inject plague bacilli into the body through a hypodermic needle? If so, what would be the volume required to be injected? Would it be potent enough to induce plague and lead to death? The doctors had other technical queries to clarify too.

The reply came four days later. Yes, the death had indeed been unnatural, induced artificially. As suspected, it was 'homicidal death', or murder. Doctors were even more baffled to learn that the bacilli wasn't even available in Kolkata. The Haffkine Institute for Training, Research and Testing in Mumbai was the only place in India from where it could be procured.

Amarendra's friends were outraged, especially because they could do nothing to prevent the death, despite knowing that Vinayendra had long tried to harm him. The pang of guilt and anger led them to visit senior officers of Kolkata Police's detective department right after his passing.

They narrated the chain of events in the presence of the Pandey family lawyer. They didn't have any proof or any documentary evidence to lodge an official complaint, but surely some unofficial snooping could be done on Vinayendra and Dr Taranath Bhattacharya?

An unofficial investigation started. Once the Tropical Medicine report came in, an official complaint was lodged by Kamalaprasad with the Tollygunge police station against five persons—Vinayendra Chandra Pandey, Dr Taranath Bhattacharya, Dr Shibapada Bhattacharya, Dr Durga Ratan Dhar and the unidentified person who had injured Amarendra with a needle at the railway station.

When Vinayendra learnt that a First Information Report (FIR) had been lodged against him, he tried to flee. But he had long been under police scrutiny, and was arrested that night from a train at Asansol railway station. Dr Dhar was arrested the following day, Taranath a day later, on the morning of February 18. Dr Shibapada Bhattacharya was able to escape arrest for the longest time, and was finally picked up on March 24.

The man who had caused Amarendra the grievous injury, however, could not be found. The short man wrapped in a dark shawl—where *was* he? Vinayendra later admitted that he had, in fact, sent him to Purna cinema hall to identify his brother. Bonobala's recollection of the man had been precise—but alas, it had been too little, too late.

Vinayendra gave the police various addresses for this man, each a different one whenever he was asked. Yet, the killer could not be traced by the police despite every possible effort, including releasing his sketches to the public.

There remained two possibilities—one, he would have been offered a huge sum of money to leave the state for some destination which even Vinayendra did not know of. Two, Vinayendra could have sent another person to kill him in order to prevent getting blackmailed in future. It is more likely that the latter is true.

Vinayendra's statement before the police would make detective thrillers seem flat and bland narratives in comparison. Imagine a young man of thirty chalking out a meticulous and diabolical plan to kill his younger brother by inserting bacteria into his body! In Saradindu Bandopadhyay's Byomkesh Bakshi stories, gramophone pins aimed from a bicycle bell, and porcupine quills are used as murder weapons. But the ingenuity of Vinayendra's murderous plan was much more evil, no doubt about that.

As the details unravelled, the police understood that Vinayendra had started planning the murder right from the day Amarendra asked for his share of the property on turning eighteen. After a failed attempt to kill him using Tetanus serum on pince-nez glasses, Vinayendra was on the lookout for something more reliably fatal. He took Taranath as a partner in the crime.

Taranath wasn't even a doctor—he had just pretended to be one. He worked as a research assistant in a laboratory called Calcutta Medical Supply Concern on Cornwallis Street and was therefore familiar with diseases and how viruses and bacteria worked on the human body. The plan to use the plague bacteria as the perfect murder weapon had sprouted from Taranath's head.

But how had they managed to procure the plague bacilli? Who gave it to them?

The Haffkine Institute for Training, Research and Testing, originally named the Plague Research Laboratory after its founder, Dr Waldemar Mordecal Haffkine, was established in 1899 in Mumbai's Parel area.

Taranath sent a telegraph to the organization introducing himself as a diploma-holder in tropical medicine researching bacteria-borne diseases. He pretended to need the bacilli for his research. The Haffkine Institute replied that only a request backed by a recommendation from the surgeon-general of Kolkata would be taken seriously enough to deserve a detailed examination on the part of the institute.

But why should anyone write such a recommendation for Taranath? This was a serious setback to the murder plan.

Enter Dr Shibapada Bhattacharya and Dr Durga Ratan Dhar. Vinayendra paid them good money to help in his plan to eliminate his step-brother. Dr Bhattacharya wrote a recommendation praising Taranath; he justified the plague bacilli's requirement by mentioning that the research had great potential. The endorsement however, had no impact. The Haffkine Institute turned it down.

Vinayendra was strong-willed and unbending in his plan, and every rejection made his resolve stronger. Perhaps he had even taken a fancy for this plague bacilli plan, for he began to explore other devious means to procure the injection from the same institute, instead of planning out some other way to kill his brother. He travelled to Mumbai several times and roped in two doctors from the Haffkine Institute. For days, he splurged on them, arranged for their entertainment in the very expensive Hotel Sea View.

The doctors were smitten by the money. Without any official record or proof, a vial of live plague culture from the institute was quietly sneaked out and handed over to the foursome on 7 July 1933. The duo from Mumbai also introduced Taranath to the Bombay Plague Hospital as a bacteriologist, where he used the sample to conduct tests on white rats until convinced of its effectiveness.

That's how the bacilli was procured and eventually injected to murder twenty-year-old Amarendra. A murder most foul, a murder most rare not just in pre-Independence India, such a plan would be considered unusual even now.

Kolkata Police's sterling performance in conducting the probe was praised by the judge in his verdict. Sub-inspector Sarat Chandra Mitra was the investigating officer when the case was taken up, and eventually Inspector M.L. Rahman continued with the probe.

Since it was impossible to track down the man who had inserted the needle into Amarendra's arm, it was essential to prove the motive with compelling arguments and collating circumstantial evidence. Only then would the chain of events become evident before the court and guarantee punishment for the accused. But this is easier said than done—only an investigating officer knows how difficult it is to present a case in this manner!

Proving the motive was simple though. It was obvious that Amarendra's death would directly benefit Vinayendra. Collating circumstantial evidence was the tough part. Investigators had to make sure it was strong and foolproof. Vinayendra's travel documents to Mumbai, his hotel bills, his handwriting in the hotel register, proofs of his visit to Haffkine Institute, Taranath's telegram to the institute, Dr Bhattacharya's recommendations to them, tracking down the store from where the white rats had been purchased, recording statements of the owner of this shop and so on—all this evidence was compiled. The Mumbai Police Commissioner extended all help and support, and would often discuss the progress of the case with his Kolkata counterpart.

Not unexpectedly, Vinayendra spent an exorbitant sum to fight the battle in court. But it did not help. The lower court ordered death by hanging for Vinayendra and Taranath. Dr Dhar and Dr Bhattacharya were acquitted. The case then moved to the higher court where Vinayendra's punishment was toned down; he was ordered lifetime imprisonment and exile to the Cellular Jail in the Andaman and Nicobar Islands. The judge mentioned in the order that the case was 'probably unique in the annals of crime'.

The case sheets also document how Vinayendra had assured Taranath while making grand preparations for the murder—'No one will know who had pricked the pin. What can the police do if they can't even find the murderer? Simple!'

Only, it wasn't really so simple after all!

PIECING TOGETHER A PUZZLE

The Belarani Dutta murder case, 1954

Tollygunge police station. Case number 116. Date: 31 January 1954. Indian Penal Code Sections 302 and 201: murder and causing disappearance of the evidence of offence.

30 January 1954. It must have been five-fifteen in the morning. Or maybe just five-thirty...

Dawn had melted into morning, the crisp winter breeze was soon going to be broken by the first warm rays of the sun. Shops in Kalighat refugee market would take a few more hours to open. The cleaners though, were up even before the break of dawn. How would they manage to scrub and sweep the place clean after the deluge of people arrived! So they always started off early, though their movements were still torpid and would turn into a tizzy of fervent activity only later in the day.

One of these sweepers noticed three newspaper-wrapped packets outside a toilet near the Keoratala crematorium. Sweepers and cleaners are accustomed to the refuse around them, and he would probably have given an indifferent shrug and dumped them somewhere. But experience had also taught him to spot the difference between garbage and... what *was* it?

The newspaper covering was torn around the edges, and when the sweeper peeped to see what was inside, he let out a yelp of terror. The package was tied with a coconut coil rope, there were marks of dried blood on the newspaper, and protruding from it were human fingers!

A crowd gathered in no time. The Tollygunge police station was informed. Officers came down and had to first clear out the crowd that had been looking intensely at the packets and scrutinizing them. Then they opened the packets, one after the other. They contained two arms that went up to the elbow joint—palm, fingers, wrist and forearm ending at the elbow. All of these had been chopped into pieces. The newspapers used were the November 21 edition of *Jugantar.*

30 January 1954. Afternoon.

The guard at Kalighat Park had just finished his lunch. Like every other day, he was strolling around the trees in the languid winter afternoon. Suddenly he froze, eyes transfixed on something behind the trunk of a mango tree. What was lying amid the thick bushes and weeds? Four newspaper-wrapped packets, tied with coconut coil ropes. Filled with curiosity, he tore open the newspapers in a swift movement, mindless of the consequences.

What he saw inside threw him into a fit of hysteric fear. Shrieking and running amok, the trembling guard's behaviour immediately drew the attention of the pedestrians walking by. Within a couple of minutes, nearly a hundred people had gathered around the packets. In one there were dismembered body parts—two legs from the knee to the sole. In another, the upper portion of a woman's body chopped into three portions. In the third, there was a head with eyes gouged out, ears, lips torn off, facial skin peeled off—all of this had been done with an obvious intent to make the face unrecognizable. Only a few strands of hair were stuck on the head. In the third packet was a full-grown dead foetus, perhaps a few days or hours before birth.

Officers from theTollygunge police station rushed again, this time to Kalighat Park, even as the early morning's unusual discovery had hardly sunk in. Officers from the homicide department of Lalbazar, headquarters of the Kolkata Police, rushed there too.

All four packets had been made using *Jugantar* newspaper—the editions of 21 November 1953, 10 January 1954, 25 January 1954 and 26 January 1954 .

The savagery of this deed was so horrifying that everyone—from the crowd that had gathered, to the policemen who were collecting the packets and other evidence—were shaken.

The park was searched thoroughly. Out came another packet which contained two portions of two thighs. The newspaper that it was wrapped in? No points for guessing that it was *Jugantar.*

27 February 1954. Past midnight.

The interrogation room of Lalbazar, Kolkata Police's headquarters. A man in his mid-thirties sat on a chair, completely fatigued by the impact of a marathon interrogation. The questioning had started around evening and showed no signs of coming to an end. The young man, though, had managed to remain unperturbed by the difficult questioning of the first few hours—he had denied everything.

This is how every difficult case pans out. The accused does not admit to the crime in the initial hours. But he is allowed to say whatever he wants to in order to defend himself. He is not countered, there are no arguments. The investigators keep noting down the statements, unresponsive, their deadpan expression giving no hint of what's going on in their mind.

After a while, complacency sets in because the person being questioned becomes confident that his lies are being taken for facts. The real game of wit takes off from there. The investigators now begin to draw his attention to the innumerable loopholes, lies and contradictions in his narrative. There is nothing he can do now to keep the truth hidden any longer.

That's exactly what happened that night. The man's tenacity was wearing out, his energy had been sapped dry, and worse, he was turning into a nervous wreck—all of this evident from the tiny specks of perspiration that had started to dot his forehead. His dogged perseverance was beginning to wear out.

Samarendra Nath Ghosh, officer-in-charge of the homicide section, had by then figured that the much tried and tested method was reaping great results. He would just need to wait a little longer. Finally the man gave in. 'Sir, I killed her. I cut her into pieces. There was no other way.' Saying this, he hid his face in his hand and rested his head on the table in front.

Samarendra felt the thrill of relief, but gave no indication of this. Instead, he picked up a glass of water from the table and extended it to the man. 'Here, drink some water. The rest you can tell me leisurely.'

The night had passed. It was almost dawn.

~

In recent times, there have been many cases of gruesome murders in different parts of India and abroad, all of which were widely reported by the media. We know about these cases from television channels and the Internet. Some cases have been the subject of films and daily soaps.

However, documentation and evidence indicate that a case such as the Belarani Dutta murder case was rare at that time anywhere in the world, for the primitive and savage violence it exhibited.

The case had obviously created a sensation throughout Kolkata. Its ripples may have faded with the passage of time, but even to this day, the Belarani Dutta murder case is considered the rarest of the rare cases in criminology research.

After the body parts were retrieved, the Kolkata Police Commissioner didn't waste time in handing over the case to the detective department of the Kolkata Police, a specialized section that had some of the best investigators in the country. Samarendra Nath Ghosh would head the probe.

On the day of the post mortem, on January 31, doctors tried to piece together some sort of a semblance of a human body. It took them seven to eight hours to give it a shape that closely resembled a female human form. There were two reasons why the corpse on the table stood out—one, the woman's feet were unusually large. Two, there was a deep cut mark on the left thigh.

The doctor presiding over the post mortem was unequivocal about the cause of death—by a sharp object near the neck, which in medical parlance was said to be 'anti-mortal and homicidal in nature'. The other wounds—there was a large number of them—had been caused after death, what is called 'post mortem injuries'.

Now the police moved on to the most difficult part: to find out who this woman was. Tracing the identity of the victim was obviously imperative if they had to find who the murderer was. But it was not going to be easy. The facial skin had been peeled off and the face severely mutilated.

But the investigators were not giving up so easily. They got in touch with Dr Murari Mohan Mukherjee, who headed the plastic surgery department of Kolkata's Karnani Hospital. Dr Mukherjee, who lived in Chinsurah of Hooghly district (about seventy kilometres from Kolkata) was a top doctor in the field.

Dr Mukherjee got down to the job with a mix of hope and trepidation. He used plastic surgery on the face of the corpse to get a hint of her face before it had been disfigured. The doctor's craftsmanship was stunning—he made a countenance out of a mutilated head severed from the body. But putrefaction had set in, and critical changes were taking place in the muscles and tissues, so the result wasn't as good as Dr Mukherjee would have wanted it to be. This was probably the first case in India where the police resorted to plastic surgery—one of the reasons why the Belarani Dutta murder case investigation still stands out in the history of criminal investigation in the country.

Pictures of the face taken after plastic surgery were published in newspapers, asking the public for help in identifying her. But there was no response, and no progress in the investigation even after a week. No one seemed to know of the woman.

After twenty days, the corpse kept in the morgue of Nil Ratan Sircar Medical College & Hospital, had to be cremated. Keeping samples of hair and bones, the body was cremated as per procedure.

By then, the Kolkata Police had conducted a thoroughly professional reconnaissance—hundreds of people who lived or had passed by the areas where the body parts had been disposed off were questioned. Information was sent out to police elsewhere in West Bengal to track down possible 'missing persons' complaints. But there was no worthwhile lead anywhere.

A month passed in this way. It was the last week of February, and still no progress had been made. When there are no positive results despite the best efforts of investigators, a despondency starts to creep in. 'It's all right. That's hardly my fault. I tried enough. So many cases remain unresolved...' such is the refrain playing in the mind.

But Samarendra was not one to give up easily. His assiduousness was comparable with German footballers—not Brazilians or Argentineans. His patience and perseverance made him believe it was possible to win even when he was on the verge of defeat. And he preferred courage over investigating flair.

It is perhaps true that fortune favours the brave and those who refuse to accept defeat. For them, the tiniest pinprick of light can signal a flash of hope.

On February 25, around nine-thirty at night, Samarendra was on his way home after a long, tiring day. He was fatigued and in low spirits due to a cough and cold. Travelling in his office vehicle between Tollygunge and Rash Behari Avenue, it struck him that he should buy a bottle of cough syrup. As the car approached Russa Road, he found two medicine stores standing cheek by jowl. A man outside the Royal Medical Store was downing the shutters, while the other one, South Medical Pharmacy, was open. He asked the driver to stop the car.

The run-down store had nothing to impress customers. The shelves were nearly empty and only a few strips of medicine and bottles were strewn around. The only employee who sat there fitted in perfectly with the surroundings—bored and displeased. It was only when he saw a customer stepping out of a police vehicle that he decided to come out of his stupor.

'I want a cough syrup.'

'Let me see if I can find one, Sir.'

After a few minutes of searching, the man replied. 'I can give you medicines for fever and headache. The cough syrup stock needs to be replenished.'

'So what's the point of keeping a shop like this open? Why not shut it down? Where's the owner?'

'Unfortunately, Sir, he hasn't dropped by even once in the past one month.'

'I see! That's the reason. What's his name? Ask him to shut shop.'

'His name is Biren Dutta, Sir. I have sent word for him many times. He is usually here every evening. This is the first time I am not seeing him around for such a long interval.'

Unable to find the cough syrup, Samarendra got back to his car and asked the driver to start the car. Only, the conversation kept playing in his head—*He hasn't dropped by even once in the past one month. This is the first time I am not seeing him around for such a long interval.*

Samarendra asked the driver to turn around. Many questions were niggling in his mind now, and he needed to clear up his discomfort if he were to return home peacefully. Actually, Samarendra was never content—whenever he did not go out of the way to clear his doubts, he thought of it as laxity on his part.

'Run and get me the address of the shop's owner,' he told his driver.

55/4/2 Turf Road. It was near Shambhu Nath Pandit

Hospital. Samarendra's energy was running low after a hard day's work and a nagging cough but he found it hard to resist visiting the place immediately.

As expected, the room was under lock and key. The neighbours informed Samarendra that Biren Dutta had lived here for many years now. He had been staying there with his wife Bela and their six-year-old son. A heavily pregnant Bela had been taken to Shishu Mangal Hospital in January-end, Biren had told them. But the neighbours had neither spotted him nor his son since January 30.

The information was enough for a sudden adrenalin rush. Only investigators who have cracked difficult cases know the sudden throb of excitement that runs through every vein when it is evident that the chase is leading to the right trail.

It didn't take more than half an hour to confirm that no one by the name of Bela Dutta had been admitted to Shishu Mangal Hospital in the past one month. The mystery was beginning to unravel.

Officers of the homicide department now delved deep to fish out this invisible character. His name was known, as was the shop he owned, and his residence. Moreover, the neighbours had described him in great detail. It was impossible that this man will not be tracked down now. Everything Biren Dutta had ever done in his life came to the police's knowledge in just twenty-four hours.

Apparently Biren Dutta had another address on Harish Mukherjee Road not too far from Turf Road. This place was put under police watch.

In the early hours of February 27, a man was seen emerging from 102A Harish Mukherjee Road, his face covered with a shawl. He was tailed for a few paces, then a bit more, until he reached Kedar Bose Road. There, he was stopped by a plainclothes policeman.

'Are you Biren Dutta?' he asked suddenly, catching Biren unawares, not giving him the opportunity to think of another name to bluff the policeman.

'Yes... but why do you ask?'

'Is Bela Dutta your wife?'

'Yes... but... why do you ask?'

'Just answer what I ask you. Where is she?'

'What can I say? Such a shameful thing... she has eloped with her lover.'

'Get into the car. We are from Lalbazar. The rest we'll discuss there.'

Biren Dutta, aka Bechu. Age 34. His childhood had been spent in a village near Budge Budge, in North 24 Parganas, a district bordering the north of Kolkata. His father, a sub-inspector in the West Bengal Police force, passed away when he was only a year old, and his mother died a few months later. His sisters Abha and Kanak were married and lived in Andul (in Howrah district, adjoining Kolkata), and Kolkata respectively.

With both his parents dead, Biren had to stay on in the village with his grandmother, and he was admitted to a school there.

He had two cousins (sons of his father's younger brother)—Nabani and Jyotindra—who lived in Kolkata's Chandranath Chatterjee Street, in the southern part of the city. When he was eight or nine years old, Biren's cousins brought him to Kolkata and admitted him to Ramrick Institution.

It would be absurd to suggest that Biren was 'studying' in school. Not only were his grades poor, he also bunked classes regularly, spending the entire time watching adult films, smoking and drinking. The furious cousins yelled, a few slaps landed on his cheeks, and he was warned but this only resulted in the wayward adolescent Biren, who was then in class eight, to stomp out of the brothers' home. He landed in the house of his sister Abha, in Andul.

Abha's husband owned a medicine store, so Biren ran errands and did some work relating to this business. Between 1934 and 1944, Biren stayed with his sister and brother-in-law in Andul.

However, his cousin Nabani, who had initially brought him to Kolkata, still held a soft corner in his heart for their 'Bechu'. He was in regular contact with the cousins and often visited Abha's home. During one such visit, he found Bechu's disposition a bit too ruffled, and his heart filled with inexplicable love and pity for his cousin, Nabani instantly decided to bring him back to Kolkata. Biren was twenty-four years old at that point.

Abha's husband, too, was affectionate towards Biren. Now that he had left for Kolkata, and wasn't by his side, his heart ached for the young man. He had bought a medicine store, South Calcutta Pharmacy, on Russa Road, around this time, and he now gifted the store to Biren along with all legal documents.

Back from Andul, Biren started living with cousin Nabani all over again. By then, Nabani's daughter Kamala was a sprightly young woman of seventeen. Kamala and Biren fell head over heels in love with each other. It was perplexing, mystifying—what they felt for each other—and they could not stay apart.

However, this was not the kind of relationship that was going to be accepted by the family because Biren was

Kamala's uncle—a close blood relation. Knowing that they were never going to get to be together, Biren and Kamala decided to elope. They rented a room on Sadananda Road, not too far from Nabani's house. Nabani made repeated attempts to separate the two, but no amount of sermonizing worked. It only led to heated arguments. Nabani's love for Biren had caused him more pain than he could have foreseen. When he realized that matters were too far gone, and his own daughter had surrendered herself in love, Nabani decided to withdraw himself and hoped this would somehow reduce at least his own suffering.

Nabani's decision to not file a police complaint against his cousin was based on the apprehension that such a step would tarnish his name and social prestige, rather than succeed in separating the young lovers.

Biren and Kamala started a new life in their Sadananda Road home. He gave her a new name—Belarani. She wanted their union to be legal and pleaded with Biren for a registered marriage. But he had always been like a recalcitrant teenager and got a thrill flouting what he was asked to do. He had put sindoor on the parting of her hair—a palpable and undeniable evidence of marriage, according to his thinking, but beyond that he did nothing. Young Belarani, giddy with love, accepted this as her fate. They identified themselves as husband and wife to the neighbours and within a couple of years they had a son, Bathindranath Dutta, their dear Boton.

After Boton's birth, they moved to the address on Turf Road. Bit by bit, Biren's relationship with Bela turned lukewarm. There was new excitement in his life now. It was Meera. Biren soon married the girl, daughter of Saroj Kanti Basu, resident of Srikrishna Lane. This time, as if to prove his devotion to Meera, Biren opted for a registered marriage. He took the plunge in mid-1948, without breathing a word about Belarani to Meera.

The only persons who knew about the existence of the two women in Biren's life were his sisters and brothers-in-law. They had never quite accepted Biren's marriage with Bela, and therefore gave tacit support to his marriage with Meera. Biren's registered marriage with Meera would eventually lead Biren and Bela to separate, they hoped.

For the first two years after marriage, Meera stayed with Biren's sister in her Goabagan house. During this time, she gave birth to a girl, though the newborn died within a couple of days. For a while Meera was in a different world, she was so numbed with pain. Then she gathered herself and asked Biren to find a place just for themselves. How could a woman have her own home and family in someone else's house?

Finally, Biren acceded to her repeated pleas. He rented a small room on 102A Harish Mukherjee Road. In 1953, they had a son.

Biren lived a life of artful duplicity. He had become accustomed to bluffing those around him on a daily basis. Turf Road and Harish Mukherjee Road were just a few hundred metres apart. Yet, for months he made sure Meera and Bela didn't know about each other's existence. He would visit the Turf Road home and have lunch with Bela, while Meera thought her husband's busy work schedule had led him to have a quick meal at the Y.M.C.A. canteen. He would spend most nights at the rented room on Harish Mukherjee Road with Meera and their son, while Bela was told that he had to make frequent trips outside Kolkata to purchase consignments of medicines.

Biren was quite without conscience, a charlatan who led a double life with near perfect ease. Had it not been for the dearth of money, Biren would possibly have pulled it off till the very end. He also had a natural talent for acting in theatre and jatra that had been his passion since childhood. Whether it was his natural talent for drama and trickery in real life that had made him a good actor on stage, or if his acting skills helped him out with his trickery in real life, it is difficult to say. Biren had acted in small plays staged in his neighbourhood during his childhood days. Later, he started visiting the film studios of Tollygunge such as New Theatres and befriended several producers and directors of Bengali films of those days and acted in at least six of them.

One of these six films was *Kamona*, the second film of Bengali matinee idol Uttam Kumar. The other films in which Biren acted included *Naari*, *Mohakaal*, *Shubhoda*, *Nishkriti* and *Paap-er Pothey*.

Paap-er Pothey—the road to sin—had a literal significance in Biren's life. His friends in the film studios introduced him to races, gambling and sex workers. His already muddled life now got murkier. He lost all inclination to look after the medicine store, and left it entirely in the care of employees. Naturally, this soon affected the business. But with two households to run, this dearth in money led to a major crisis.

He tried to pull through somehow. But matters reached rock-bottom with the news that Bela was going to have a second child. It drove him insane.

What was going to happen?

'I could not take it anymore, Sir. My business was under severe distress. I had to take loans. And I had grown tired of leading a double life, lying to both Meera and Bela. I was scared of getting caught. Meera was getting suspicious, very soon Bela too had begun to question me about my long absences from home. Why stay outside most nights, she would ask. When I heard she was going to have another child, I shuddered at the thought of the additional expenses it would involve. Then I thought it best to get rid of her. Believe me, Sir, there was no other way.'

Biren's narrative would be cross-checked later, but as he confessed, no one interrupted the flow of his words. The investigators let Biren go on, letting him blurt out more and more details.

'I pretended to be angry. I told her this is not my child. You've taken advantage of my regular absences. At first she cried, then we had a big fight over this.'

Only his son Boton, then six years old, was now in the way of committing the murder. But Biren's fertile imagination came up with a plausible story to tell Meera. He told her a friend and his wife had died in a road accident leaving behind their only six-year-old child. If Meera wouldn't mind, could he bring the orphan home? Meera was filled with such pity she could not refuse.

On 27 January 1954, Bela was then nine months pregnant.Biren got back home from the pharmacy around 10.30 p.m. and found Boton sleeping soundly. Bela served him dinner and Biren ate silently. Suddenly, he told her gruffly, 'I am not going to spend money on a child that isn't mine.' As soon as he hissed at Bela, her patience ran out. 'Do you think I am not aware of your flings?' she retorted.

He had been waiting to strike, and now he started raining blows on her. He dashed for the kitchen, got hold of a sickle and struck her on the neck. As if one strike was not good enough to kill her, he kept striking her. She was killed instantly. As her lifeless body slumped to the ground, he emptied a cupboard, and put her body inside. Then he washed away the blood, but not before he had taken off all the gold jewellery on her—six pairs of bangles, ring and earrings. Then he calmly went to bed.

The following morning, January 28, Biren began to implement the plan exactly the way he had chalked it out. Benu Roy was a close friend of Bela and lived alone in a room on the first floor of the Turf Road house. She adored Boton, and used to spend a large part of the day with the child.

'I called Benudi in the morning and told her that Bela had to be urgently admitted to Shishu Mangal hospital late in the night, and the delivery could happen any time. Would she have trouble keeping Boton in her care for some days? Benudi happily agreed. Boton inquired after his mother in the morning. I told him she had been admitted to the hospital and would be back with a baby brother or sister soon.'

Relieved that these humdrum things had been taken care of, Biren left for his medicine store for the day's work. Bela's body lay locked inside the cupboard. He had worked out his plan till the last detail by now, including how he would dispose of the body. If the police could not find the body, how would they ever track him down? Around 9.30 in the evening, the employees of the pharmacy left for the day, and Biren got to work on his plan.

He picked up some *Jugantar* newspapers stacked in his shop and headed straight to the Turf Road home. What happened next, Biren told the sleuths in a calm, dispassionate voice:

'I took out Bela's body from the cupboard. Then I chopped off her head with a sickle, severing it from the body. Next, I cut off the ears, nose, hair, hands, feet, chest, belly—all of it, one after the other. I peeled off the skin from her face too. After I had wrapped each of these with *Jugantar* newspapers and tied them up with coconut coil ropes, I put them back into the cupboard, and locked it up again. The room was flooded with blood and an obnoxious, putrefying smell, so I had to wash the room several times with phenyl.'

This part of the work done, a relieved Biren went off to sleep—now for two nights in a row with the body inside the cupboard. He woke up in the morning and left for the pharmacy as usual, stayed at work all day and got back home at night. He took out all the packages, put them in two big, strong nylon bags used when shopping for the family's ration, then he hired a rickshaw and went near Kalighat Park, but stopped a few paces away. Alighting from the rickshaw, so he wouldn't have the rickshaw puller around to witness anything, he dropped some of the packets into the park. He dropped off the remaining packages near Keoratala crematorium, outside a public toilet, on the way home.

On his return to the Turf Road house, Biren did another round of washing and cleaning of the floor. This time he also removed blood stains splattered here and there and cleaned the cupboard thoroughly.

Next morning, he bumped into Benudi while leaving for work.

'How is Bela doing? I so want to visit her!'

'No, Benudi. There is no need for it. Perhaps the delivery will happen tonight. Her pressure is fluctuating, and doctors have kept her in a solitary cabin. She'll be home in no time.'

The experienced actor delivered the same lines with equal ease to the other inquisitive neighbours. Over the next few days, Biren took all of Bela's jewellery to the Harish Mukherjee Road house, informing Meera it was a surety against some money a friend had borrowed. Then he disposed of Bela's clothes, cosmetics and other objects of daily use into the Tolly's nullah, a water channel traversing the south-western part of the city that was actually more of a sewer channel.

He took Boton from Benudi's custody and went to the Harish Mukherjee Road home. By then, Meera was anxiously waiting for the unfortunate orphan boy whose parents had died in a road accident.

The Kolkata Police assembled witnesses and proofs with a lot of care. Bela's jewellery was retrieved from Harish Mukherjee Road, the sickle used to murder and chop Bela to pieces was found in the Turf Road house. There were strands of her hair stuck on the sickle and on the phenyl bottle. Dry stains of blood samples were collected from the floor.

Forensic report confirmed these as human blood, and that the strands of hair belonged to a woman. It also confirmed that the hair on the sickle and those on the phenyl bottle belonged to the same person. These were all considered very important evidence in court.

In order to prove that the deceased woman was Belarani, the investigators obtained documents to show that she was pregnant. Combing the Turf Road residence, sleuths got hold of a ticket dated 24 November 1953 for a check-up by a gynaecologist at Shambhu Nath Pandit hospital.

This, then, was evidence that Bela had visited the doctor in pregnant condition.

Biren had an odd habit of collecting old newspapers. Yellowish and tattered newspapers were likely to be found in his pharmacy. All the newspapers were seized from the pharmacy and as expected, once they were arranged in chronological order, newspapers from some days were missing. Only those that were used to cover Belarani's body parts were missing. This circumstantial evidence was of major significance, the court observed during the trial.

Belarani's relatives were informed about the murder immediately after the matter came to light, and after Biren's arrest. They had long remained out of touch, but the brutal murder of their girl, that too with such savagery, left them in a state of disbelief and shock. When her father, uncle, brother, sister, all gathered to meet the investigators, they noticed one more thing. The post mortem report had mentioned that the murdered woman had had unusually large feet, and now the investigators noticed the same kind of feet on all her relatives.

Could this prove that the murdered woman was Belarani, aka Kamala?

The Deputy Commissioner of the detective department wrote a letter to Dr S.S. Sarkar, the illustrious and acclaimed professor of Calcutta University's Anthropology department, inquiring about this. Photographs of Kamala's feet, along with tracings of her father and uncle's feet were sent to Dr Sarkar. Would he be able to indicate if they were from the same family, the Deputy Commissioner wanted to know.

The legendary Dr Sarkar studied the traces and the photograph, and finally the much awaited letter from him reached the police. Yes, Dr Sarkar wrote, they were indeed from the same family. This further established the identity of the murdered woman. The investigators were inching towards a foolproof chargesheet.

All this would have been unnecessary had DNA tests been in vogue. But this was 1954, and DNA tests came to be used in criminal cases only some decades later in 1986, in England's Leicester, in connection with a rape and murder case.

The final blow for Biren was Belarani's mother's statement. Remember, there was a deep cut mark on the left thigh of the murdered woman's body? Looking at the photograph of the thigh shown to her by investigators, Bela's mother was in tears. She recalled that her little Kamala had hurt herself when she was eight years old, and the injury had left a permanent mark on her thigh. Who could have offered a better testimony than a mother?

Finally the chargesheet was filed in court. That chargesheet was so watertight that it can serve as a lesson for investigators even today on how to frame such a document.

The defence lawyer's argument in the Alipore Sessions Court was that the unidentified woman was not Belarani at all. They stated that she had eloped with her secret paramour—a claim that was proved otherwise in a series of intense court hearings. Arguments and counter-arguments went on for six months. Documents that recorded circumstantial evidence and forensic tests finally led the court to announce its verdict—Biren Dutta was to be hanged till death.

The higher courts, first the Calcutta High Court, then the Supreme Court, gave the same verdict. Biren Dutta was hanged on the morning of 28 January 1956, for the murder of Belarani, or Kamala.

Italian sociologist Cesare Lombroso, who is known as the father of criminology, was the first to suggest the possibility of trying to delve into the murkiest corners of criminal minds by merging science and anthropology. It was on this foundation that the research on criminal psychology is based.

As one leafs through the fragile, yellowish pages of the case diary of the Belarani Dutta murder case, it seems some cases can never be understood within the paradigms of information and research. How can one understand or explain the savage mind of Biren Dutta and the barbarity of the killing? There is not much it can be compared to in terms of the method of killing and the brutality it involved from the time.

In his book, *Beyond A Boundary* (1963), renowned Trinidad historian C.L.R. James (1902-1989) had written, 'What do they know of cricket who only cricket know?'

The mind of the criminal can be described similarly—how much can be known of the mind from the outside? Whatever glimpse is available superficially hardly indicates what goes on in the truly murky depths.

THE SKULL BENEATH THE PICTURE

The Pancham Shukla murder case, 1960

South Port police station. Case number 174. Date: 21 March 1960, Indian Penal Code Sections 364 and 302: kidnapping or abducting in order to murder, murder.

'I did it in the heat of the moment, Sir...in a fit of mad frenzy.'

'That's what people say when they get caught.'

'No, Sir. It's not that... trust me!'

'Trust, doubt, all that will come later. First, tell me where is the body. Come on, quick! I don't have time to waste.'

'I have buried it, Sir.'

'Where?'

'Underneath the muddy bed of a lake.'

'Lake? Which lake? Where? Tell me everything. Otherwise, we have all the ammunition at our disposal to extract the truth, hope you know that?'

'I'm telling you everything, Sir... It's near Taratala...'

'Come on, get into the car, quick!'

A young man in his mid-thirties followed the instruction without a word of protest. The car engine roared, and it started off from Kolkata's Port area, moved through the silence of the night towards the Taratala area of south-western Kolkata.

'Where's the lake?'

'Left turn now, Sir...'

The car slowed down, its engine stopped, only the wheels kept rolling for a while, then eventually it came to a halt near a water body. It was well past midnight; the streets were deserted and barely lit. The young man, drained of all energy, the result of a horrifying interrogation session, showed the way with staggering footsteps. Police officers from the detective department tailed him, the long rubber gumboots on their feet sploshing through the mud and water, the result of an untimely shower.

'The body is there, Sir, buried underneath. I thought no one would ever find it.'

It wasn't really a lake—more thick mud with a shallow layer of water. The corpse had been embedded deep into the mud. Actually, there wasn't much of a corpse left either, it was a skeleton with bits of flesh still stuck to the bones here and there. Only a few shreds of dhuti and a torn shirt were still stuck. The jaw bones, some bones from the left rib cage, right patella, hyoid bone (connecting bones between neck and chin) had all gone missing from the skeleton, too. It was pretty much clear that water and mud had aggravated decomposition, and foxes and vultures had feasted on this lavish meal.

The torn shirt had four buttons still attached to it, the pocket showed a small red flag with a white border—the unmistakable uniform of an armed security guard of the port. A sacred white thread worn by Hindu Brahmins had miraculously remained intact. In the wee hours of the morning the entire water body was searched, resulting in some important recoveries: some jaw bones, a tiny quicklime container—a necessary accompaniment for chewing tobacco—with the words 'Om Jai Hind' scripted on it—and a foot long knife (the last was found planted deep inside the muddy bed). Was this knife the murder weapon?

~

Rows and rows of goods laden ships gently moved into the Kidderpore dock and anchored near the shore—their customary sluggish movement along River Hooghly a routine event. Pancham gazed at the stunning sight. He never tired of it—wondering where they came from, and who had sent them. He sat by the bank everyday after work, even though this invited taunts from his friends—'It's the same sight, goods come in, they are unloaded. What's there to gawp at everyday?'

Pancham remained silent. If only he knew the answer himself! When he had bagged this job of an armed security guard at the Kolkata Port several years ago and had set off for Bengal from distant north India, little did he know that this place would be so alluring! It was inexplicable.

But life here had brought its own complications and problems—specifically in the person of Ramlochan.

'I can't wait any longer, Pancham. I'll give you another week, not a day more.'

'You know how hard I am trying to arrange for the money. Please give me some more time!'

'You've been parroting these lines for the past two months. Not five or ten rupees, it's five hundred rupees, no less! I had myself borrowed it from my father. If I knew it was going to be so hard to retrieve the money, I would not have loaned it to you!'

'Same here. If I knew you would drive me crazy with

stern reminders every single day, I wouldn't have borrowed from you either. Is it possible to arrange five hundred rupees at the snap of a finger, unless one decides to loot someone?'

'Go ahead then, loot somebody, but give me back my money. Surely you don't expect to earn some just by counting ships?'

Pancham now lost his cool.

'I shan't return your money. Not a pice. There's no written agreement, no proof that I took any loan from you. Go ahead and do whatever suits your fancy.'

'Really? I know how to extract it from you, by the way. If you pinch my cash, I'll ensure that it gets impossible for you to keep your job.'

'Huh! Get lost! I'll see what a big shot you are!'

A little later, however, a dark cloud of melancholy descended on Pancham. He shouldn't have been so angry. It was true, five hundred rupees was no small sum. But, shouldn't a friend understand how hard he was trying? Had both his parents not fallen ill at the same time, Pancham wouldn't have needed so much cash. What should he do now? Should he sell his ancestral land? Would his father and his uncles agree to it?

Pensive, Pancham stood up and began to walk towards his living quarters as memories of home, of his wife and two sons filled his mind. He hadn't been home for so long! He decided to approach the superintendent next week to ask for some days off to go home. The superintendent appreciated his hard work, so he would possibly agree to grant the leave. He would go home and propose selling off the ancestral land this time. How long could he go on carrying the burden of debt?

Better to sound an early warning here in order to avoid readers' disappointment: unlike detective novels, there's no edge of the seat suspense here while unravelling the mystery, nor the thrill of finding out who was the murderer from among a group of suspects.

The accused wasn't even found by a police investigator through the stroke of a brilliant brainwave. In fact, this case was rather easily solved compared to some of the more complex ones that Kolkata Police sleuths have handled. And yet, the Pancham Shukla murder investigation is a momentous one—it remains a milestone in the Kolkata Police's glorious history. In fact, this case has a special significance in the history of India's major police case studies.

This will also, quite naturally, indicate the crucial difference between criminal cases of fiction and actual, real incidents investigated by police forces.

Investigation involves two important parts. First, zeroing in on the person who committed the crime, leading to their arrest. Fictional investigations mostly conclude at this point. Whether it is Satyajit Ray's Feluda, Saradindu Bandopadhyay's Byomkesh, Nihar Ranjan Gupta's Kiriti Roy, or Hemendra Kumar Roy's Jayanta-Manik duo—all iconic detectives of Bengali fiction—the sleuths keep readers engaged with suspense till the point of crime detection. However, there is a second part, a reality beyond this. For the real sleuths of Lalbazar, the job *after* the arrest is of paramount importance too.

This work that comes after crime detection ensures punishment for the accused. This is an apparently dull, monotonous process stripped of exciting discoveries. However, not treading this path would mean that the humongous effort of hounding out the accused would go waste. It is understandable that detective fiction writers aren't keen on this bit because it is flat and largely soporific from the outside.

But here comes a twist in *this* tale—the post detection episode of the Pancham Shukla murder case is far more interesting than catching the murderer.

Pancham got back home to his tiny, derelict living quarters by 7.30 in the evening, every single day. On March 10 he didn't return. Night led to dawn, dawn gave way to a new morning, but there was no sight of Pancham. His brother-in-law, who also worked in Kolkata Port and lived in adjoining quarters, scouted around for him patiently all through the day, but when he wasn't back till evening, he lodged a missing person's diary with South Port police station that night.

The police follow a routine procedure on receiving missing complaints. Everything was followed by the book—wireless messages were sent to police stations, accidents in which victims hadn't been identified were tracked, a photograph of the missing person was obtained from relatives and publicised. But Pancham remained missing.

His friends and colleagues were interrogated and one of them disclosed to the police that Pancham had recently been planning to start a garments business with a friend, Ramlochan. A security guard in the port mulling a cloth business? The sleuths thought it required further probing. Ramlochan's address was found without difficulty. He lived alone in a three-roomed flat in Taratala, in the city's south-west.

The door to his flat was found locked. Neighbours said that they hadn't spotted Ramlochan since the morning of March 11. The police then deployed their men in plainclothes to keep a round-the-clock vigil outside his house without raising anyone's suspicion.

After a few days of agonized wait, Ramlochan surfaced in the early hours of March 21, trying to enter his flat secretly, wrapped in a shawl.

Ramlochan Ahir. Approximately thirty years old.

After about two hours of interrogation at the police station, he admitted to killing Pancham. Every gruesome detail of the murder, all the skeletons in the cupboard, came tumbling out in no time.

Ramlochan belonged to an affluent family. Though he was not a Bengali, his family had lived for several generations in Kolkata. His father and grandfather were garment merchants. Unlike those in earlier generations, Ramlochan was a risk-taker keen on exploring other business opportunities, and even wanted to export goods abroad. His interest in export led him to frequent the dock area, and that's how he had come in contact with Pancham. Acquaintance had quickly led to thick friendship.

Pancham's parents, who lived in their ancestral home in Bihar, had fallen ill. He needed a lot of money rather urgently for their treatment, prompting him to approach his wealthy friend. Ramlochan responded to the crisis as a friend would have. He gave Pancham five hundred rupees as loan. In the Sixties, it meant a lot of money.

Around that time, Ramlochan had invested some money in setting up a car spare parts business. But it was a fledgling venture, and he needed to pump in more funds to make it look reasonably good. Thus, he soon needed his money back and asked Pancham to repay the loan. Pancham, however, had no money to return, and requested for some more time.

Ramlochan grew increasingly impatient—he required the money urgently. Therefore, every day he sent rude reminders to his friend about how much he needed the cash. Matters reached a flashpoint in the last week of February when he issued an ultimatum to Pancham.

'I want my money back within three days. Else, I'll go to the police.'

'Go ahead. There is no written agreement. I'll tell the cops I haven't taken any loan from you. Simple!'

'Is that so? Do you think you can get away with pinching my cash?'

'Didn't I just tell you to go ahead and do whatever your heart desires?'

On that day—perhaps at that very moment—a terribly vexed Ramlochan came to the conclusion that Pancham had lost his right to live. Once he was convinced he had taken the right decision, it was just a matter of executing the plan.

Within a week of the showdown, Ramlochan put his devious plan into action. He had carefully planned every detail. Pancham should have no hunch or suspicion of the dark scheme—about that Ramlochan was cautious—and so he took on the role of a repentant friend seeking forgiveness.

'You know what, Pancham, I have been so depressed since that fight with you. Please don't take it to heart, brother!'

'Same here. Even I am down since that day. Have I ever said I won't return your money?'

'Oh, come on! Let it be. I have a brilliant plan.'

'What?'

'The car spare parts business is not getting anywhere. I know the garments business like the back of my hand, and it would be wiser if I concentrated on it. Someone has agreed to pump in some cash. He'll drop in at my place day after tomorrow. Why don't you come by for a short while?'

'But what am *I* going to do there?'

'Why don't you put in some labour for a few hours in the business after work? You are having trouble returning the cash, this way you can pay with your labour! There's no hurry, you repay the loan in this manner over a period of time. What's the point in fighting over this?'

It was a proposal Pancham could not refuse. This was a glorious opportunity to avoid paying the cash. In fact, there was no place for him to earn so much money at that point. So the idea suited him perfectly.

Pancham went straight to Ramlochan's place at the scheduled hour—at eight the following evening. Considerable time was spent drinking and chatting, and around 10 p.m., Pancham began to feel a nervous anxiety.

'I feel sleepy. When will your friend drop in?'

'No idea. He should have been here by now. Maybe he is stuck somewhere? Let's just walk down to the lake. It's rather humid in here. The lake is just a stone's throw—let's go sit there for about fifteen minutes in the cool breeze; you can leave after that, and I'll come back.'

'Hmm. All right!'

The two walked down to the bank of the shallow water body, and had a chat engulfed by the thick, shadowy darkness of the night. Not a word came from anywhere other than their low, muffled whispers. Around 11.15 p.m.,

Pancham, his voice tired and low, said, 'I should take your leave now.'

He stood up, preparing to leave. The moment he stepped forward, Ramlochan took out a sharp knife he had kept hidden inside his shirt all along, and stabbed Pancham from behind. Pancham, though strong and well built, was totally unprepared for this deadly assault, and clearly outmanoeuvred. By the time his mind and body were prepared to fight the suddenness and shocking brutality of being attacked by someone he had trusted as a friend, Ramlochan had already planted the knife into him repeatedly. Pancham dropped dead on the ground, bleeding from the chest, abdomen, neck, throat—innumerable stab wounds all over his body.

And then?

'I had planned all of it ahead. Accordingly, I buried the corpse in the muddy bed of the water body. I dropped the knife into the water. My father had got it from Delhi a few years ago. Imagine, first Pancham took my money, he wasn't able to return it, and then he showed such reckless disdain instead of gratitude! I couldn't take his arrogance, Sir, I lost my cool. I committed a grave mistake, Sir, out of a raging anger that burnt my inside, it destroyed all my senses…'

~

Anil Banerjee, Inspector with the Kolkata Police's detective department was assigned to the probe. The case had been resolved, the accused had admitted to his crime. But, the proof? Where on earth was the proof?

Section 27 of the Indian Evidence Act 1872 says: 'How much of information received from accused may be proved—Provided that, when any fact is deposed to as discovered in consequence of information received from a person accused of any offence, in the custody of a police officer, so much of such information, whether it amounts to a confession or not, as relates distinctly to the fact thereby discovered, may be proved.'

The skeleton had been retrieved following the statement of the accused. The knife—the weapon of offence—had been found. Relatives of the murdered persons had identified his dhuti, shirt, quicklime container. What more could one ask for?

Anil-babu, an experienced officer, knew that the job was still incomplete. The skeleton had been found, but it required conclusive proof that it was indeed Pancham's. Anil-babu was anxious that this was not going to be easy. So he began to seek advice from experienced lawyers. Most said the same thing—that even if the accused had admitted to his crime during police interrogation, he would definitely deny it in court. That's what happened in ninety-nine per cent of the cases.

Under the circumstances, it was highly probable that the accused would get away without any punishment, unless it was proved absolutely beyond any argument that the skeleton was indeed Pancham's. But the evidence available till then were inadequate to prove this and thus it was possible that the accused could get the benefit of doubt.

Anil Banerjee passed away some years ago. His juniors at work still speak very fondly of him, and they remember his quiet perseverance. Banerjee was not an insouciant killer like Sir Vivian Richards on the cricketing pitch, but he had the calm diligence of Sunil Gavaskar—able to survive the most unfavourable situations. In fact, he was not one to limit his work due to lack of infrastructure; rather, he wanted to try the impossible by overcoming such stifling boundaries. He was also an avid reader and enriched himself by reading up on criminal cases from India and abroad.

The lawyers' advice worried Anil-babu to no end. How would he ever prove the skeleton was Pancham's? A young man's life had been taken by brutal stabbing simply because he could not repay five hundred rupees—how could he allow the murderer to get away? No, this was unacceptable.

In those pre-Internet days, libraries were the only reliable source of information. Anil Banerjee, who enjoyed spending his spare time at the National Library, recalled reading about a similar case abroad—the investigator's dilemma and strange plight of proving a skeleton as a certain human being. Where had he read about it? Feeling restless, Anil-babu rushed to Alipore. Only the National Library could show him the direction in this case.

Yes, the library certainly calmed him down, but also excited him at the same time. A strange thrill filled his senses. Was he about to do something new in the history of the organization? Yes! He had read about this case earlier: the Buck Ruxton Jigsaw murders case!

Buck Ruxton was born in India as Bakhtiyar Rustomji Ratanji Hakim. He studied medicine and left for England, and officially changed his name to Buck Ruxton. Apparently a popular physician, Ruxton had brutally stabbed and murdered his wife Isabella and their maid, Mary Rogerson at their Lancaster home in September 1935.

Ruxton had used his knowledge as a doctor to carefully dismember both bodies into several parts, ensuring that all identification marks were removed perfectly. Then he parcelled each piece of the body parts and dropped them from a bridge into a ravine in Scotland. His objective was very clear—even if the dismembered body parts were discovered, there would be no way to prove that these were actually Isabella's and Mary's. His motive? An obsessive jealousy. Buck was convinced Isabella was having an affair. There had been many arguments over his repeated allegations and her constant denials. Isabella had left home a number of times with their children over this, and Buck had brought her back each time. But the suspicion, allegations and arguments continued, eventually leading to the brutal murder of Isabella. Mary Rogerson was murdered because she had accidentally witnessed it.

A few passersby saw the parcels from the bridge, and an investigation started. A parallel was drawn with pieces of a jigsaw puzzle: piecing together the different parts to form the two different corpses of Isabella and Mary was an arduous task for the investigators. That's how the case came to be known as the Buck Ruxton Jigsaw murders case.

A group of experts consisting of forensic pathologist Prof John Glaister and anatomy specialist James Couper Brash achieved the impossible. One, they put the pieces together to form two different corpses. And two, this was the first time ever that 'photographic superimposition' was used in an investigation. This helped in the identification of the two women. This sort of application of forensic science expertise had never been done before. Buck Ruxton was proven guilty and sentenced to death.

The sensational case had gripped the people of England for days.

The song, *Red Sails in the Sunset*, written by Jimmy Kennedy, was immensely popular at the time. Kennedy lived in Ireland's Portstewart and often watched a vessel with red sails, which is said to be the inspiration behind the song. The Buck Ruxton murder had created such ripples that people altered the lyrics of the song thus:

Red stains on the carpet/Red stains on the knife
Oh Dr Buck Ruxton/You murdered your wife
Then Mary she saw you/You thought she would tell
So Dr Buck Ruxton/You killed her as well

~

Once he had retrieved the details of the Buck Ruxton case, Anil rushed from the National Library to the Forensic Sciences Laboratory (FSL) to explore the possibility of applying in the lab the knowledge he had gained from books.

Only a handful of cases had applied 'photographic superimposition' till then, but at least it had been a successful method. That knowledge itself was enough for Inspector Anil Banerjee, who had already begun to dream of doing the same in the Pancham Shukla murder case.

Dr Nirmal Kumar Sen was then the director of FSL. Dr Sen said that tests had already determined the gender, age and height based on the person's skeleton. It belonged to a 35-year-old male of five feet six inches height. Anil asked the doctor whether it was possible to try out the photographic superimposition method to confirm beyond doubt that this was indeed Pancham Shukla's body. Would Dr Sen give it a try?

All this, of course, was required because the DNA test method did not exist as yet. This was the first time in the country that the superimposition method was used in an investigation.

What is this superimposition method? If a certain point of a human face in a picture matches with clinical precision with the same point of the same human face in another picture, it may be called a superimposition. In human bodies, these points are known as 'nodal points'. These are biological, and different for every individual. To make these two pictures match, it is first essential to make two pictures of the exact same size. Thus, a passport size photograph of Pancham Shukla's face was first enlarged to quarter size with the help of a negative. This was done to match the photograph with the exact size of the skull.

The contours of human faces are all different from each other—the eyes, nose, forehead, chin are all of varying sizes. Therefore, only if the two photographs match with complete precision, it would mean the face in the photograph and the skull belonged to the same person.

Pancham's photograph was placed below a ground glass, the nodal points were marked, the skull was placed on a stand and taken to the exact position of the photograph. Bit by bit, as every nodal point of one picture matched with the corresponding nodal points of the skull, it was scientifically proven that the photograph and the skull belonged to the same person. No doubt about that!

In a country lagging far behind its European counterparts in infrastructural support for investigation and crime detection, a skeleton retrieved eleven days after the murder matching with a missing person through an ingenious technique, was no doubt a rare and major feat. It created a sensation in police forces throughout the country.

Today, superimposition can be done at the snap of a finger on a computer. But sixty years ago, this technique was unheard of. Anil Banerjee's ground breaking work found place in the *Indian Police Journal* in a piece titled, 'Camera Identifies Human Skull'. It was rare that someone other than an IPS officer, renowned lawyer or doctor would find a place in this journal as a contributor. But the editorial board was so impressed by Banerjee's work that they chose to make an exception.

During the trial, the legal validity of this method and its efficacy as evidence were questioned, but the arguments did not hold good. The lower court ordered Ramlochan's death sentence, and subsequently the Calcutta High Court changed it to life imprisonment. This verdict was upheld by the Supreme Court of India.

It is well known that the Kolkata Police used to be compared with Scotland Yard. If a list of cases were to be compiled in order to determine why they had earned this sobriquet, the Pancham Shukla murder case would surely have been part of that list—a case whose inspiration incidentally—and funnily too!—came from Scotland.

GOODBYE, DEAR BURI!

The Debjani Banik murder case, 1983

Gariahat police station. Case number 49. Date: 30 January 1983. Indian Penal Code Sections 120B, 302, 201, 34: criminal conspiracy, murder, causing disappearance of evidence of offence, or giving false information to screen offender, acts done by several persons in furtherance of common intention.

'We are policemen... Please open the door!'

The 'please' was completely unnecessary here. Hirendralal Majumdar never pleaded with people. However, now he used the word in parenthesis hoping it would act as some sort of a mild assurance to those on the other side of the palatial door to this fourth floor flat on Gariahat Road.

Trickery was part of his job. He threw these random tricks at people knowing half of them wouldn't work. Like now. It didn't work. When four officers from Gariahat police station including Majumdar walked four floors to reach the doorstep, they found the collapsible gate locked, though the thick mahogany door behind it was slightly ajar. But now, it moved a bit and clicked shut, as if an imperceptible breeze in this otherwise still night had pushed it deftly. It was 10.15 p.m.

No one spoke. Yet, there were voices around. Whispers and murmurs of both male and female voices could be heard from behind the door. It wasn't really difficult to guess that there were, in fact, several people inside. Majumdar now hollered, 'I am the officer-in-charge of Gariahat police station, Hirendralal Majumdar. Open the door. Right. Now.' This time his sharp voice cut through the stillness of the night. It could have broken a sheet of glass into shards.

Silence. The lights inside the flat went off, as if the same trickster of a breeze had blown them out. Majumdar had never allowed himself to return empty handed, nor was it permitted in his job. And therefore he was not one to be embittered by these increasingly daring attempts by the inhabitants of the flat flouting his commands.

Now, it was time for the final warning. 'Do you want me to break open the door?' the OC inquired only with a dash of provocation, not letting the surge of indignation inside him reflect in his voice.

A few seconds' pause and he knew he would now have to send a man from his team as a messenger to the nearby fire station. And so he did, asking fire department officials to rush to the fourth floor of 26 Gariahat Road with all the equipment required to break open an iron collapsible gate and a thick wooden door. But before the officer left, Hirendralal Majumdar whispered something into his ears.

Ten more minutes. The siren of a fire tender and the fast approaching tapping of footsteps along the flight of concrete steps signalled to Majumdar that the fire services team had arrived. Along with them, the police officer had brought along four neighbours who were to act as witnesses to this entire episode. You would be foolish to not have witnesses in an episode such as breaking open the door while the residents were putting up a stiff resistance with their resolute and cold silence.

The inhabitants would plead innocence, and therefore

Majumdar was well prepared even before he had stepped into the flat. As he and the other three officers banged on the door, the OC had already thought of a courtroom scenario where this case would be fought. And it had clicked in his head right then: there should be witnesses to this episode. And who better to act as witnesses than neighbours? Therefore, while the junior officer was sent to inform the fire station, Majumdar had whispered into his ears to bring along some neighbours too.

Gariahat doesn't sleep early, unlike other affluent neighbourhoods. When the ebullient shoppers have tired themselves out, taken buses or trams home and the shops have downed their shutters, the sidewalks still continue to bustle with those engaged in late-night adda sessions at paan-bidi shops. The adda sessions under the pretext of discussing literature and music on sidewalk perches over tea and cigarettes can often sink dangerously into idle prattle. But you can never take the Bengali out of his adda. Unless of course, the diversion is far more captivating. And on that night, such a diversion was waiting to take place.

While shops in Gariahat shut by 10 o'clock at night, most paan-bidi shops remain open till midnight. With Gol Park-Dhakuria to its south, Ballygunge-Park Circus to the north, Bijan Setu-Ballygunge station to its east and Rash Behari Avenue and Chetla to the west—the flow of people, cars, buses and trams become sluggish, but continue till late into the night. Gariahat crossing has a life of its own different from any other part of the city.

In minutes the crowd began to swell. Additional forces were sent from Lalbazar control room—the Kolkata Police's headquarters approximately eight kilometres away. It didn't take them too long to reach Gariahat given that the roads were largely empty around that time.

The fire officials took some time to break open the two gates. By then, everything had gone eerily silent. It was pitch dark inside. Not even whispers were seeping through.

Majumdar, with his retinue of police and fire services officials waiting behind him, lit a torch, its stream of light moving in an unsure stagger through the sprawling hall. Three women stood there, fear written clearly on the contours of their faces. The officer-in-charge now thundered: 'What's going on here? Why weren't you opening the door? Do you think we have come down for a chat at this hour of the night?'

This is the story of Debjani Banik. A woman in her early twenties who was brutally murdered in the house of her husband and in-laws—a place that could never be her own home.

The telephone at the Lalbazar Control Room had rung exactly at 10 p.m. that night. The duty officer had picked up the phone and heard a male voice speak what seemed to be a well rehearsed line, in a curious mix of concern and coldness: 'Send your men to the Baniks' house on Gariahat Road. They have killed their eldest daughter-in-law. If you don't rush, they might dispose of the body.'

The phone had clicked and disconnected. Sometimes, such preternatural things do happen. Like a boon or a blessing, this telephone call had led the policemen to the Baniks' house on Gariahat Road. In the days before caller line identification (CLI) devices arrived, which now inevitably disclose telephone numbers, it was impossible to trace the caller at that time.

The Baniks' house was approximately 300 metres from

the Gariahat police station. But if distances were to be measured in terms of time—as they often are to those with a natural predilection for time rather than physical spaces—it would take someone three minutes to cover it on foot. A vehicle would take even less time. And therefore, merely minutes after the call to the Lalbazar Control Room, Mr Majumdar was banging on the door to the Baniks' flat.

The Baniks' place turned out to be bigger than a football ground. It was, in fact, a triplex. The fourth, fifth and sixth floors were internally connected through staircases. The enormous front door to the fourth floor through which Hirendralal Majumdar had entered led to a spacious hall with several rooms on either side. Each of these rooms had their own private balconies. In one corner of the hall stood a temple enclosed within glass walls.

The search operation began. Both the upper floors were found to be locked. The police decided to start off with the fourth floor. In one of the rooms, three children were found sleeping on a bed. An old woman lay asleep in another room. In a third room, a woman in her fifties, a pitiable picture of ill health, lay like a spectre on the bed with her eyes closed. But she was perhaps not asleep. A boy of around twelve years was found sleeping in the fourth room. The kitchen door was under lock and key.

It was like a canvas with only half the picture drawn. There were too many jagged edges. Too many secrets waiting to be unravelled.

'Where are the men?' an officer asked the three women who stood there, fixed to the ground, visibly shaken. But it was evident that they were still putting up a brave front, and tactfully holding onto their silence.

'We heard male voices from outside. Where are they?' the officer demanded to know. But the stoic silence of the women could not be broken. 'Is Debjani Banik the eldest daughter-in-law here? Where is she? Call her!' Still, not a word.

By then, the officers were beginning to sense a familiar stench. It was not strong enough to be discerned from outside, nor on immediate entry. But as soon as they got accustomed to the dull ordinariness of the rooms, the stink began to unsettle them. Doctors and police officers are all too familiar with it: the stench of rotting human flesh.

They stopped dead in their tracks, directing their search operation to the trail that led them to the stench—it was coming from a room in the north-eastern corner of the flat. Nose covered with handkerchiefs, the officers took a quick glance around the room. It was empty except for a neat bed. The bedcover had been folded under the mattress without a single crease and was disconcertingly immaculate.

The room had an adjoining balcony, but its path had been blocked with a heavy iron swing placed obliquely as if it had been carefully planted to impede movement. The group of policemen lifted the iron swing with some effort and found a foldable single bed piled with mattresses, blankets and comforters. Everything was taken out and checked. Nothing.

The space under the bed, too, was stuffed with clothes—deliberately stacked to block every inch of breathing space. These were now taken out, one by one. And from under the bed rolled out the body of a young woman. Her sari and blouse clad body was bloated and rotting, muscles and flesh had stiffened as a result of rigor mortis setting in. Blood from her nose and mouth had drenched her saree, but had now dried. And there, they could all see the deep, dark mark resulting from something wound tightly around her throat and neck.

The three women were called into the room. 'Do you know her?'

The answer was an audacious 'No' in unison.

Now, the young boy had to be woken up. 'Who is this woman?' asked an officer.

The boy burst into sobs. 'That's Boudi.'

'Her name?'

'Debjani. Debjani Banik.'

Senior officers from Lalbazar reached the Baniks' house within an hour or so. Deputy Commissioner (headquarters), Deputy Commissioner (detective department), Deputy Commissioner (south division) and several officers from the Kolkata Police's homicide section were all heading towards Gariahat Road that night. Sujit Sanyal, Sub-inspector of the homicide section, was going to lead the investigation.

The death of a housewife generated a lot of lurid interest among people in Kolkata and elsewhere in West Bengal. Was it because newspapers were captivated by the sensational nature of the crime—the murder of a young housewife, whose father and father-in-law were both rich businessmen of the time? Was it because the woman had been murdered in an affluent residential area such as Gariahat? Were they moved by the picture of the demure young bride whose hopes and aspirations were doomed to be dashed? The striking image of a young woman being throttled into silence amidst the busy goings-on and cacophony of the surroundings was spine chilling.

Whatever the reason may have been, even in the days before the onslaught of electronic media, the Debjani

Banik murder case was front page news in leading Bengali newspapers like *Anandabazar Patrika* and *Jugantar* for months. Even during the lengthy courtroom trials.

People unfamiliar with this part of south Kolkata walking down the road from Gol Park towards Gariahat are likely to be shown this eleven-floored multi-storeyed building with, 'That's Banik-bari. *That* Banik-bari, remember?' The episode has conferred upon the house a cruel notoriety.

Who were those three women? What did they disclose on being arrested? How had the men escaped the house? How were they caught?

This is no whodunit. There are no twists and turns, mysteries and clues that will lead us to the killers of the young Debjani. Many people may even recall that her husband, father-in-law, brothers-in-law and sisters-in-law were involved in the murder. Some may even remember the names Chandan and Chandranath, her husband and father-in-law, respectively.

This narrative is about the circumstances that led to the death of the young woman, the dramatic events leading up to her murder and the events that followed it. Debjani Banik's death may, in fact, be considered one of the worst episodes of violence against women in the country.

The Banik family of Gariahat was rich and prosperous from their main business of tea gardens. Several other businesses had helped them accrue enormous riches over the years. The Banik-bari—the eleven-storied Banik house—had been built by the patriarch, Chandranath Banik. He had rented out some and had sold the remaining flats on the ground, first, second flats and third floors of the building to government and non-government organizations for use as office space or to individuals for residential purposes. The patriarch, nearly sixty years old, himself occupied the fourth floor, where he lived with his family in a 10,000 square feet flat. The fifth and sixth floors were under his possession, and four more floors above it, going up to the tenth floor, were under construction.

Chandranath's wife had taken to bed because of an illness and led a largely inactive life. He had nine children—five daughters and four sons. The eldest daughter Kalyani lived with her husband and in-laws in Kasba, not too far from Gariahat. Jayanti lived in Jalpaiguri district, about 600 km from Kolkata, and Chitra had been married to a resident of Serampore, a small town in Hooghly district, approximately thirty kilometres from Kolkata. Sumitra and Bitra, the two youngest daughters, weren't married and lived in the Gariahat house with their parents.

Chandan was Chandranath's eldest son. This gave him a superior status compared to his other siblings, apart from insurmountable power, honour and prestige. That's what eldest sons were meant to be. Chandan was married to Debjani, the only daughter of Dhanapati Dutta from Burdwan's Notungunge, approximately 100 km from Kolkata. The marriage had been arranged by the elders of both families and in all likelihood, Debjani and Chandan may not have even met once before they were married. They had three children—sons Babu and Tabu, and daughter Mamoni—all of them less than eight years old.

Chandranath's other sons were Ashish, Asim and Nandan. Ashish was married to Rupa, and the couple had a daughter, still a toddler. Asim was unmarried, and the youngest Nandan, was a student of class seven, only twelve years old.

There were five domestic helpers in the house. Chaitanya, the cook, who had been employed for many years, lived in a small room on the landing of the third floor. Jadu, a young man, lived in a room similar to Chaitanya's, adjoining the staircase on the building's second floor. His job was to accompany Chandranath to the market every morning, wash utensils, and run errands all day. Urmila, who came twice daily to the house, morning and evening, cleaned and swept floors, washed clothes and assisted in the cooking. There was also a young woman Pushpa, around twenty years old, who looked after Debjani's children. A twelve-year-old girl named Shanti looked after Ashish and Rupa's toddler.

The Dutta family, Debjani's maiden family, was based in Burdwan district. The Duttas, too, were extremely wealthy, Their money came from their rice mills, petrol pumps, fish cultivation. In addition, they owned large swathes of cultivable land and a number of properties in Burdwan district. Dhanapati Dutta and his wife Sudharani had three sons—Debdas, Biprodas and Ramdas. Their only daughter, the darling of the family, was Debjani, the youngest and the most beloved. The brothers called her Bonu, her parents gave her the pet name, Buri.

The Dutta and Banik families had arranged the marriage of Chandan and Debjani in August of 1975. It was indeed a child marriage for Debjani was just fourteen, and Chandan had turned twenty. Dhanapati Dutta had showered his daughter with gold and enormous riches. She was, after all, his only daughter, his greatest treasure. He wouldn't allow the Banik patriarch to feel that the marriage of his eldest son had not lived up to his expectations.

The first three years of the marriage passed like a dream

for the child bride. Boro-Boudi, as she was called, was a favourite of the brothers and sisters-in-law. Boro-Bou—the eldest daughter-in-law—was adored by the in-laws.

The cracks began to appear around July-end in 1978. Dhanapati Dutta had come down to meet his daughter, when Chandranath and his wife told him, 'The time has come for our Chitra to be married. We would want her to be married to your eldest son, Debdas.' But Dhanapati had to politely turn them down. 'If only your proposal had come earlier! You know that Debdas is to be married to Kumkum, daughter of Asansol's Harishadhan Ghnati. The wedding is in August. Now, I cannot break my word. It is too late.'

Chandranath Banik's jaws turned taut, he and his wife left the drawing room without uttering another word. Dhanapati waited for them to return, fidgeting uncomfortably as he talked to his daughter. Being her father, he saw himself in a disadvantaged position. The father of the groom was supposed to enjoy his arrogance. Not him. Despite the odd discomfort he felt at not getting the appropriate hospitality and respect at his daughter's home, he spent some time talking to Debjani, then left for Burdwan.

Very soon, Dhanapati Dutta came down to Banikbari again to invite them for his son Debdas's wedding. Chandranath Banik asked Dhanapati, 'Isn't Dr Mrinalkanti Bishnu a relative of yours?' In the three years that Debjani and Chandan had been married, both families became somewhat acquainted with each others' distant relatives as well. 'Yes,' replied Dutta. 'He is close to our family. My brother's wife has a sister. Dr Bishnu is her husband.'

Chandranath Banik made it clear that if Dr Bishnu

came to Debdas's wedding, then the Banik family would not attend it.

'Why? What is the matter?' Dutta enquired with concern and panic, trying to make sense of this sudden whim.

It came to be known that before Debjani and Chandan's wedding had been fixed, the Banik family had been discussing a possible match between Chandan and Dr Bishnu's niece. No match could be finalised however, without looking at the bride—an elaborate ritual in which the groom and his family members visited the girl's house. They enquired after the girl's qualities and looked at her from all possible angles to make sure that not just her father's money and social standing, but, she too, would be talked about at the wedding.

However, the day the Banik family was to visit Dr Bishnu's niece, Chandranath Banik was a good seven to eight hours late. Worse, he had gone only to inform the family that they weren't keen on this match. But without even looking at the girl? What right did the arrogant gentleman have—no matter how rich he was—to insult them? Dr Bishnu and Chandranath Banik had a heated argument. Since then, Chandranath Banik could not stand the sight of Dr Bishnu.

Dhanapati Dutta sat there, heard the story, and left. But on the day of Debdas' wedding, Chandranath Banik found that his wish hadn't been honoured. Dr Bishnu was present.

'How dare you invite me to your son's wedding only to insult me!' he thundered at Dhanapati Dutta, who tried to plead with him saying how embarrassing it would be to not invite a close relative. But Banik was not one to see reason. 'Your daughter will never come to your house again,' Chandranath informed Dhanapati and walked out, making it clear that Debjani was now part of the Banik family and her actions and freedom—or the lack of it—depended entirely upon decisions taken by him.

The third step in this growing chasm between the two families was over the purchase of a water body in Burdwan district. Dhanapati Dutta had spent a huge sum of money on it, but was told by Chandranath that he, too, had placed a written official proposal, a bayna, to purchase it. Dutta was a seasoned businessman, not one to be bogged down by hollow threats. He demanded to see the bayna-nama, or the official document that would prove that Chandranath had indeed placed an order. But no such document was forthcoming from Chandranath, and this incident, too, led to mild arguments.

The growing differences between the two families began to impact the way Debjani was treated by her in-laws. The treasured Boro-Boudi and Boro-Bouma began to be ridiculed with sharp jibes from nearly everyone in the family, accompanied by occasional slaps and thrashings from husband Chandan, who was also complicit in this.

Debjani would earlier visit her parents once every two months, and write to them regularly. Now, the strain was evident—she would visit them once in a blue moon, after endless pleading with her husband and in-laws. Her letters became more and more infrequent and then stopped.

Debjani, however, continued to display her tenacity—the way thousands of women do in the absence of alternatives. Without higher education or jobs, where will those dependent on their husbands go in the face of repeated blows and beatings. And what would her actions do to her father's reputation?

The situation built itself to a dramatic climax in mid-

1982 over the purchase of a cold storage in Burdwan. Chandranath had bought it on a bank loan of several crores of rupees. His other robust businesses had plummeted, and thus even the operation of the cold storage was erratic due to lack of adequate funds. The bank loan had to be repaid in instalments, but the Baniks could not do this on time, and the bank slapped a 'demand notice' on the Baniks. Chandranath asked Dhanapati to pay at least twenty-five per cent of the sum that the Baniks had loaned. Dhanapati was under no obligation to do so, but the Baniks used his daughter's presence in their home to pressure him.

After gauging the situation, Dhanapati said he could manage to give rupees ten lakh at the most. Twenty-five per cent of the bank loan was seventy-five lakh, and it was too high a sum for him to pay. Chandranath's belligerence had by then hit a new low—he abused Dhanapati to no ends. The veneer of courteous behaviour that had so far remained as a cover to the underlying tension was now blown away. The relations had turned openly hostile.

Debjani's physical abuse grew more aggressive, as did the verbal and mental torture.

By then, Chandranath's wife had become nearly bedridden. Chandan's beatings increased, and Debjani's father-in-law, sisters-in-law and brothers-in-law began to refer to her as alokkhi—a reverse of the Hindu goddess of wealth, peace and prosperity, Lokkhi. It was her negativity and damaging presence that had cast a dark shadow over the household, Debjani was told everyday, the reason why the cold storage business did not take off. 'The very sight of this alokkhi brings bad luck. Now, our entire day will be spoilt.' These were the comments directed at Debjani almost every morning. She was shaken.

The cook, Chaitanya's heart ached for Debjani. When she wrote letters to her parents he posted them in secret for her. In these letters she indicated how much she was suffering.

My dear Ma, I have been enduring their torture for the past five years. I can't, anymore. I won't stay here any longer. Please send Baba here. I want to be with you all. If I stay there for a month, I'll feel so much better! I am writing this letter in secrecy, and sending it through Chaitanyada. They don't let me talk to Baba over the phone. When I talk to him, they stand by my side so they can hear every word I say. I feel like crying. Your son-in-law is not a good man. He is always abusing me, he hits me in front of the others. One can't stay on like this. Do ask Baba to come and take me home. I can't take this anymore. With pronam, your Buri.

Whenever Dhanapati came down to meet Debjani, he had to wait for hours in the drawing room for a few minutes of conversation with her, and even that was in the presence of her sisters-in-law.

Around twenty days before the Durga Puja of 1982, several members of the Dutta family were in Kolkata's Sealdah area at a relative's place. They were visiting the house of a prospective bride for Dhanapati's second son, Biprodas. Dhanapati himself was in Burdwan. In the afternoon, he received a call from Debjani at his rice mill, 'Baba! I have been horribly beaten up by your son-in-law today!' Unable to utter a word more, she broke into a whimper.

A nervous Dhanapati immediately called up his relative's house in Kolkata and told his wife Sudharani, 'Go to Buri's house right now. Don't waste any time.' The Duttas rushed to Gariahat from Sealdah.

It may have taken them less than an hour to reach Gariahat, but at the Baniks' house, they had to wait for forty-five minutes before they could meet their beloved Buri. When she came in, she was accompanied by her sisters-in-law. They couldn't have a word with her in private. Sudharani's heart sank when she saw Debjani's swollen elbow. But mentioning it would make things difficult for her daughter. So she cautiously placed her request before Chandranath, 'I want to take Buri to Burdwan for some days.'

It was turned down forthwith.

After a lot of coaxing, Sudharani's valiant attempts paid off. She was asked to be patient. 'Chandan will travel to Tripura on work soon. Take her to Burdwan then,' Chandranath finally agreed.

Some time later, her brother Ramdas did take her to Burdwan for a few days. There, Debjani narrated to her parents the brutality of the tortures, and about her impossible sufferings. Dhanapati and Sudharani did what most parents were wont to do at that time, and what many perhaps continue to do today. They advised Debjani to be resilient. 'We'll talk to Chandan. Things will be fine, try and adjust a bit more, my Buri'.

The Boro-bouma of Banik-bari knew that the situation was outside her control. She had been told before she left the house that if her father did not pay twenty-five per cent of Chandranath's Banik's bank dues, Debjani would never be allowed to visit her parents' house in Burdwan again. Dhanapati tried to reason with his daughter that it was an impossible proposition. He had already promised to pay ten lakh rupees, and now he said he would try to arrange some more.

Chandan arrived in Burdwan to bring Debjani home. Her parents didn't let their resentment show. They pleaded with Chandan to not hurt their daughter. Yet, instead of shame and guilt, he erupted into anger and swore he would never let Debjani visit her parents again.

Little did Debjani's parents know then that it would be the last time their beloved Buri was visiting them. No parent could have imagined in their worst nightmare what was waiting to happen.

As she touched her father's feet before leaving her home, seeking his blessings, he put his hand gently on her head. An overwhelming ache singed Dhanapati inside, but there was no way he could have guessed that the next time he would see her, it would be her cold, lifeless, bloated body in the morgue of Kolkata's Medical College Hospital.

A few days before Mahalaya—the day that heralds the coming of Durga Puja—Dhanapati's son Debdas went to Banik-bari with Puja gifts. Debjani's parents had sent clothes for all the Baniks. But the Banik patriarch refused to accept the gifts. An insulted Debdas returned home. Dhanapati knew in his heart then that this Durga Puja would not bring any joy for their Buri.

He was right. The torture increased several notches; Debjani was secluded from the main goings-on in the Banik family. She was made to live separately. In mid-December, Chandranath and Chandan visited Burdwan in connection with the submission of certain documents relating to their cold storage. There, they bumped into Dhanapati's trusted employee, Hrishikesh Ghosh.

Chandan took Hrishikesh to their car in which Chandranath Banik was sitting. His words were cold and cunning.

Hrishikesh Ghosh in his statement to the police said, 'Chandranath-babu told me that he would take revenge. "Tell your babu, that I am seeking revenge—a revenge that will burn him all his life." I said, "Why are you telling me all this? Whatever you want to say, go tell him."'

Chandranath had made up his mind by then.

28 January 1983. There was Satyanarayan Puja at Banikbari that day. The house was full of the warm chatter of invited relatives—a deceptive exterior to the festering wounds inside. Ashish and his wife had gone to his in-laws' place some days ago. The others—Debjani's sisters-in-law, brothers-in-law and their children—were all in the house.

Among the housekeepers, Jadu, Urmila and Shanti were present. The cook, Chaitanya, had gone to his native home three days earlier and Pushpa was on leave. She had gone to her home in the Sunderbans.

At 8.05 a.m., a heated argument between Chandan and Debjani broke out in their sprawling drawing room. Incensed at her audacity to argue he pulled her by the hair and dragged her to their bedroom. Everyone in the family witnessed this. Her screams and cries from the room made it clear to the others that she was being beaten up. No one protested, no one uttered a word. Instead the relatives concentrated on preparing the shinni—the traditional Satyanarayan Puja offering made with a mix of milk and flour, sweetened with dry fruits and nuts.

8.30 a.m. A tearful and seething Debjani ran out of the room and called her Burdwan home. Her eldest brother Debdas was at the other end. The Duttas were preoccupied with preparations for a discussion concerning a property in the court that day, when the phone rang. Debdas heard his sister crying, 'These people will kill me! Dada, please come here right now and take me home!'

The colour ran out of Debdas's face. He was shaking. Dhanapati took the telephone receiver from his son's hands and could make out that Chandranath, who had already snatched the telephone from Debjani, was abusing her. Debdas took the phone from his father again and told Chandranath, 'Please Kakababu! Please don't hit Bonu anymore. We will leave for Kolkata this evening, and we'll bring her home.'

Chandranath had hung up. The Duttas decided to rush through the urgent work in court that day so that they could start off for Kolkata by that afternoon. Who knew that the decision to leave in the afternoon, instead of immediately, would make such a momentous difference?

The Satyanarayan Puja got over. The Baniks devoured the specially cooked food made for the occasion. Debjani, who had turned into an alokkhi, was neither allowed to go near the shrine, nor given food. The relatives—including the Baniks' elder daughters Kalyani and Chitra—left in the afternoon.

Around dusk, Chandranath was pacing up and down the hall, seething, seeking to take his revenge. His sons Chandan, Asim, Nandan and daughters Jayanti, Sumitra and Bitra were also in the house.

Chandranath's wife, his mother, Debjani and the children, were in separate rooms. Jodu and Shanti went about their work as usual. Urmila had just completed her hectic round of morning and afternoon chores and had stepped out of the flat. She was expected to get back for the evening shift.

4.05 p.m. Chandranath and Chandan entered Debjani's room. Immediately after, her agonizing shrieks were heard from outside the room, making Jodu and Shanti nervous.

They ran out of the kitchen and made a dash for her room. They loved Boro-boudi, and feared something terrible may have happened to her. Sumitra stopped them near the hall, 'What are you two doing here? Come on now, get back to work.'

Debjani's cries stopped after some time. At approximately 4.30 p.m., Jodu saw Asim, Jayanti, Sumitra and Bitra go into Debjani's room. The day was far from ordinary, the movements of the people, Debjani's cries, the oddness of the quiet that had filled the flat now—everything was unusual, felt Jodu and Shanti. The valiant attempt on their part to probe further was met with furious resistance this time, again from Sumitra, 'Hadn't I asked you to concentrate on your work? What are you doing here?'

Jodu and Shanti returned to the kitchen. By then they had seen enough—Boro-boudi was dangling from the ceiling fan, a sari tied around her neck.

At around 4.45 p.m., Dhanapati and Debdas were preparing to leave for Kolkata, when the telephone rang. Dhanapati's heart sank. What could it be this time? Debdas picked up the receiver. It was Chandranath, his voice calm.

'Doesn't look like you've started off for Kolkata yet…'

'We are just about to leave…'

'I suggest you drop the plan. I'll be in Burdwan on work tomorrow. I'll meet you at your Durgapur petrol pump?'

'May I speak with Bonu?'

'Bouma and Chandan have gone out to watch a film. Don't worry, she is doing fine.'

The Duttas weren't fully convinced about this abrupt transformation. They worried about it all evening. What could be the reason behind Chandranath's oddly gracious behaviour? Regret? Repentance? That was the only possible explanation. Perhaps they had worked out a compromise? It was just a matter of a few hours, thought Debdas and Dhanapati. The next day, they would discuss it, and bring Debjani back.

Meanwhile, a strange gloom had descended on the Banik-bari. It had nothing to do with the darkness of the evening. The crime had been committed, but how could one hide or remove every trace of it? It was difficult to remain steady and work it out till the last detail.

Shanti and Jodu often stayed back in the house at night. That day, Shanti was sent to Urmila's room. Jodu, who often slept in the kitchen, was asked to spend the night in the space that was allotted for him on the second floor. But before he left, Jayanti issued a firm warning, 'If a word of this goes out, you will be accused of theft and you'll lose your job. Remember, you'll die hungry. Don't have any doubts about that.' When Urmila arrived for her evening chores, she found the collapsible gate locked. On ringing the bell, Chandranath came out to inform her that she could skip the chores for this part of the day. 'Come back tomorrow,' he instructed.

So what had exactly happened to Debjani? She had been slapped, kicked, assaulted with severe punches and blows. But even that had not been revenge enough. Chandranath hit her on the head with a wooden pole, leading to massive internal haemorrhage. Then, in an effort to make the murder appear a case of suicide, her body was tied to the ceiling fan with a sari.

The door to Debjani's room had been locked, and the children were told that their mother was unwell and needed to rest. You stay in another room, their father had said. They trusted their father too much.

As evening gave way to night, the enormity of the murder and its ramifications began to sink in. What if the suicide theory was not taken at face value? They dithered on this, different opinions and arguments were weighed against each other. Around midnight, the Baniks decided to hide Debjani's body under a bed kept in the balcony.

The following morning, 29 January 1983, Chandranath and Chandan left home around 10 a.m. with a suitcase. They went to the Indian Overseas Bank at Gol Park to withdraw one lakh rupees in cash. From there, they went straight to the chamber of their family physician, Dr Ajit Kumar Banerjee, a doctor they had known for years.

They needed a death certificate, Chandranath told Dr Banerjee. How about writing this death certificate? The doctor said it was impossible without looking at the body.

Chandranath confidently opened his suitcase stacked with bundles of cash. 'How much do you want?'

It didn't have the desired impact on the doctor. The doctor snapped the suitcase shut and said with a wry smile on his face, 'No matter how much you offer, this is beyond me...' With that, he politely asked them to leave.

Chandranath was now unsure what his next step should be. Then he made yet another mistake in the string of goof-ups he had already committed. He decided to not leave the doctor's chamber without clearing a nagging doubt. 'Do post mortems reveal if a death has been caused due to murder or suicide?' Chandranath asked foolishly.

It was less than a moment's pause before the doctor reacted. 'Of course, it very clearly does,' the doctor said, trying his best to hide his concern. 'But why do you ask?'

The father-son duo did not bother to answer that. They turned around, left the doctor's chamber and headed straight home. Did the call to Lalbazar Control Room that night come from Dr Ajit Kumar Banerjee? No one knows for sure. We can only hazard a guess.

Jodu and Urmila were back to work as usual. Shanti and Pushpa were back from their native homes. The snubs and threats were not enough to keep them quiet, and Jodu and Shanti shared their experiences of the earlier day with Urmila. There was a death-like silence around them, as they spoke only in whispers, stewing in the still air that had engulfed them. How were they to escape from this rotting hell?

In a rare show of courage Urmila inquired from Chandan, 'Where is Boro-boudi? I didn't see her after my return.'

Chandan would neither bend nor break. 'She went off to her parents' place. Her brothers had come down last night.' The children found their mother's room locked. 'She is in Burdwan for some days. Ma will be back soon,' they were told.

Around 10 p.m. Urmila finished her work and left, and Jodu was about to leave too. Pushpa and Shanti were around, when suddenly, the bell rang. 'We are policemen... Please open the door!'

The lights were switched off. Chandranath, Chandan and Ashim took the connecting stairs to the fifth floor. From there, they used the stairs from the building's rear side—a narrow, winding, iron staircase built especially for use by cleaners—to flee. They took the gate from the rear side of the building that opened to Rash Behari Avenue. The women locked Jodu, Shanti and Pushpa inside the kitchen. 'Don't you dare utter a word to the policemen. Not even if they beat you up,' warned Sumitra.

The policemen broke open the door and entered the flat. All of Chandranath's guile was not enough to keep the crime a secret.

Where did the men escape? First, to Hoteliers Associates, a hotel on Mahatma Gandhi Road in central Kolkata where Chandranath booked a room identifying himself as Ramesh Dutta from Agartala. His sons took the names Sushil Dutta and Ashok Dutta. A day later, they hired rooms at the Sealdah Lodge on Bipin Behari Ganguly Street, also in central Kolkata. Here, he filled the registration form under the alias Gour Saha.

Over the next few days, the Debjani Banik murder case became the talk of town. In every nook and cranny of Kolkata it was dissected, discussed, speculated and argued about all through the day. Front page newspaper reports were read down to the last detail. The most proficient police teams combed the entire city, goading their sources with pictures of the three men. It didn't take too long for Chandranath to figure out that being on the run would be impossible.

He left the hotel on February 4 along with his two sons and headed for Hazra in south Kolkata (not too far from their Gariahat house), to their lawyer. Police had prior information of this through their sources, and stopped the taxi with the three men near Rash Behari Avenue crossing. From there, they were taken straight to Banik-bari. The wooden pole that was used to hit Debjani on the head was found from the office chamber on the fifth floor. The sari that had been used to tie her to the ceiling fan was found from the sixth floor of the house.

It is the police's job to prevent crimes and to unravel mysteries and secrets behind offences, move on to filing chargesheets in courts, presenting witnesses, delivering documents and articles seized as proofs. All of this is done in the hope of bringing the case to a perfect closure. It requires sharp minds, in-depth investigations, persistence and fortitude. And it needs patience to go through the long and meticulous court proceedings, to deliver evidence during the hearings, and to wait for the court's verdict. When one ruling is challenged, the case goes to a higher court. Police investigations are then brought under the scanner too—why is this part slightly ambivalent? Why hasn't that person been interrogated? Where is this person's statement? Why is the seizure list incomplete? No slip is acceptable.

And that's how it ought to be, especially when it comes to a crime as heinous as murder, and when the punishment demanded by the prosecution is death or life imprisonment. The court decides the sentence after carefully taking into consideration all these factors from every possible angle. And the court's verdict must be accepted.

The job of a policeman can occasionally be as dull and tiresome as any other profession. But once in a while, there may be a case that impacts him more than other cases. In those times, the shrewd cop works beyond the concerns of his job, not because of the critical articles newspapers are writing, nor because his bosses are asking him to push the limits.

The officers of the Kolkata Police's detective department have always been known throughout the country for their brilliant investigative acumen. But in the Debjani Banik murder case, the facts the investigation threw up, moved them to tears, and their heart ached for the young woman, making the sleuths go beyond professional demands.

Sujit Sanyal, Sub-inspector of the homicide section, led his team to ensure that the offenders got the maximum possible punishment.

Sujit Sanyal was bold, hardworking, sharp and courageous with a soft heart—exactly what is required of police personnel. He fought the case valiantly, not leaving any stone unturned. There are so many investigators such as Sanyal in the Kolkata Police force, whose stories are never told. Sanyal did not need to smoke a particular brand of cigarette to set him thinking, like fictional detectives. Sanyal's brain was working all the time. He did not need a satellite. He worked with his team of officers, and all their contributions were equally valuable to how the case was fought in the courts. In his illustrious career, Sanyal cracked many important cases, and retired from the position of Assistant Commissioner of Police.

The court proceedings began. Bitra was tried in the juvenile court, as she was not yet eighteen. The Banik family spent a fortune on lawyers, claiming Chandranath, Chandan and Ashim weren't present in the house when Debjani had died. The arrested women too claimed innocence. Murder? But it was suicide! they claimed.

Such astonishing claims would never have gone in their favour. After all, Jodu and Shanti's statements severely clashed with the Baniks' claims. The wooden pole with which Debjani had been hit had Chandan's fingerprints on it. Police got hold of the registration records from the hotels where the three Baniks had been hiding, and it matched with Chandranath's handwriting. Mostly, the letters Debjani had written to her parents were testimonials that did not leave any doubt how tumultuous her life had been, the sheer agony that she had been facing was laid bare in them.

The post mortem report by the head of the forensic sciences department of Medical College, Dr Robin Basu, cleared every possible doubt regarding the suicide theory. Debjani's body had innumerable injury marks, the strike on her head was so powerful it had cracked her skull. 'Fissured fracture on the vault of her skull and several other injuries, all anti-mortem and homicidal in nature.' Plus, the mark on her throat, which, in police's parlance is called 'ligature mark', was indicated to be 'post mortem hanging', which meant it was created after she was already dead.

Kolkata's Alipore Court announced the verdict in April 1985. Jayanti, Sumitra and Asim got life imprisonment, Chandranath and Chandan were to be hanged. This is what the verdict read: 'But the part played by accused Chandranath irrespective of his age and that of accused Chandan deserve the severest punishment enjoined by the law and no leniency need be shown to them having regard to the facts and circumstances of the case.'

The Baniks moved the Calcutta High Court. There, the verdict was altered a bit. Chandranath, Chandan and Sumitra's orders remained the same. Ashim and Jayanti were ordered two years of imprisonment. The next obvious step was the Supreme Court. The court ordered life imprisonment for Chandranath and Chandan.

After fourteen years, the three of them—Chandranath, Chandan and Sumitra—were released. Chandranath is no more. Bitra was being tried by the juvenile court, and may have been termed guilty. However, the Supreme Court ordered her release three years after her arrest.

What would Debjani have looked like? A fair, doe-eyed beauty with chiselled nose and dark hair that went up to her knees? Maybe she was. Maybe she wasn't. Was she a dark girl with a ravishing smile and a crooked nose? Maybe she was. Maybe she wasn't.

Whatever she looked like, no matter how rich her father was, if only there were people who could feel the throb of her fear, sense the desperation of her lonely battle. There was no one to hear her cries for help, and Debjani could not be saved.

BODY OF EVIDENCE

The Anurag Agarwal kidnap and murder case, 1988

Park Street police station. Case number 631.
Date: 17 October 1988. Indian Penal Code Sections 120B, 368, 384, 302, 201: criminal conspiracy, wrongfully concealing or keeping in confinement kidnapped or abducted person, extortion, murder, causing disappearance of evidence of offence.

'I repeat, Mr Agarwal, do not inform the police. Else, you'll never see your grandson again.'

'I won't, I assure you. Please don't harm him, Mr Gupta! I've already promised to you that I'll arrange the money. I'll do whatever you say.'

'Do you know where Basusree cinema hall is?'

'Yes, Hazra crossing…'

'Right. Bring your car outside the cinema hall around 7.20 p.m. Wrap the money in brown paper and tie it with a red ribbon.'

'…my colleague Dindayal Upadhyay will be there.'

'Ask him to come out of the car with the packet in hand, wait for a few minutes and then to get back inside. My man will reach him, he must give the packet immediately…'

'But my grandson… Maltu…'

'The money first… your grandson will reach you tomorrow. Hope you are sending eighty…?'

'Yes… but, if only I could talk to him once…'

‘He has been given pills…he is sleeping now.’

‘But…’

‘No ifs, no buts, Mr Agarwal. If you want to be sure your grandson is with us, my man will hand over his wristwatch to your messenger when he brings the money.’

‘All right…’

‘So there… remember, I’ll get to know if the police are informed. 7.20 p.m., Basusree. All right?’

Gulmohan Mansion, 60 Middleton Street. Flat number 43, fourth floor. The Agarwals had lived there for years. Sixty-three-year-old Devilal Agarwal was chief administrator of French Motor Car Company Limited, an automobile company. The native home of the Agarwals was in Gorakhpur, Uttar Pradesh, where Devilal’s sons Shailendra and Murarilal continued to run the family business of electrical equipment manufacturing.

Shailendra’s two daughters lived with him in Gorakhpur, but his son, Anurag, the youngest among the siblings, lived in Kolkata with Devilal. Fourteen-year-old Anurag—Maltu to family members—studied in Julian Day School on Elgin Road, in class six. Shailendra, his wife and daughters visited Kolkata occasionally.

Anurag loved living in Kolkata with his grandparents. He was the most cherished, dearest grandchild to the grandparents, and shared a special bond with grandfather Devilal. All his affection, tantrums and annoyance were directed at only one person—Dada, his grandfather. His parents often wanted to take him back to Gorakhpur, but the boy would have none of it. Devilal didn’t want to impose his wishes on his son, daughter-in-law or grandson but he was excessively gleeful all those times that Anurag turned down his parents’ pleas to take him back to their native home.

In 1988, Devilal decided to set out on a pilgrimage he had long been planning. But his wife fell ill quite unexpectedly, and instead of cancelling the trip, Devilal went alone. To take care of his ailing mother during his father's absence, Shailendra, his wife and elder daughter Sangita, came down to Kolkata. They would return to Gorakhpur only after Devilal's return.

It was October, and Anurag's school was closed for the Durga Puja holidays. Life was simpler in metros such as Kolkata at that time—there were fewer cars, no cacophony and chaos on the roads, and strictures imposed on children were far less. Pre-teenage and teenage children had a lot of free time after school and a fourteen year old was considered old enough to roam around the city with friends as long as s/he returned home by sundown. Somehow, most middle-class homes in the city had nearly the same rules for children, with only minor variations in how far from home they could venture out.

Anurag was allowed to make short trips to interesting places near his house—Alipore Zoo, Indian Museum, Victoria Memorial or thereabouts. Every time he would be back before daylight began to fade.

On October 12, around afternoon, his sister Sangita sensed Anurag's sudden absence in the house. After informing her mother about this, they checked every room, and then every corner of the house. No, he was certainly not home. The guard of Gulmohan Mansion confirmed that he had noticed Anurag stepping out of the building at around 1 p.m., a plastic bag in hand. The mother and sister were relieved to hear this. Perhaps he had gone to meet friends? Nothing unusual about that, but what upset them was the fact that the boy hadn't cared to inform anyone before leaving. Wait till he got back, he needed to be admonished, both mother and sister thought and went about their work as usual.

But when Anurag wasn't home by evening, they got anxious, even panicky. Frantic calls were made to his friends' homes all evening till late into the night. Shailendra, along with some neighbours checked all possible places that the child was likely to visit, such as Park Street, Victoria Memorial, Alipore Zoo, Princep Ghat and Eden Gardens but Anurag could not be found. The family spent an agonizing, endless, sleepless night.

In the morning, Devilal called as usual, like he did whenever he went out of town, and Shailendra broke the dreadful news to him. Devilal advised his son to lodge a missing person's complaint with the police and himself set off for Kolkata, cutting his trip short.

Shailendra followed his father's advice and rushed to lodge a complaint with the Park Street police station (on October 13). An investigation was started immediately. Officers made inquiries, sent the boy's photographs to other police stations, looked at lists of accidents in the city since the time Anurag had been missing from home.

On October 14, they received not one, but several calls from a person—one Mr Gupta—who claimed to have kidnapped Anurag. He issued grave warnings that the boy would be killed if one lakh rupees ransom was not paid within twenty-four hours. Shailendra pleaded that it was impossible for him to arrange such a huge amount of cash in such short time, that he knew no one in the city and his father was yet to return. Please could he be kind enough to grant some more time?

On the same day (October 14), at around 10 a.m., Devilal

had reached Gorakhpur and was preparing to board a train to Kolkata. The journey to Kolkata would take over twelve hours and it would be almost 11 p.m. when he reached so he decided to make a call home from Gorakhpur railway station. The news unsettled Devilal—a certain Mr Gupta had called to inform that they had kidnapped Maltu. The caller had even threatened to kill the child if they dared to inform the police.

A flustered Devilal, his hands shaking, unable to utter another word, tried his best to remain composed. What should be the best thing to do in such a situation? He advised his son to seek some time from the kidnappers if they called again. 'Do not inform the police about the ransom call,' he advised. He also asked his son to prepare to pay the ransom, by withdrawing rupees thirty thousand from the bank as quickly as possible, and pooling in the remaining amount from friends.

Devilal returned home past midnight. The house was filled with relatives, friends and neighbours, all nervous, edgy and dazed wondering what could have happened to the boy. A number of Devilal's colleagues had by then contributed as much as they were able to arrange, and Shailendra, too, had withdrawn money from the bank. After counting it all, they found that it amounted to rupees eighty thousand—still a good twenty thousand rupees short.

At nine in the morning of October 15, the telephone in Devilal's house rang again. Mr Gupta was on the other end.

'What have you decided? I don't have much time...' the voice was filled with cold impertinence.

'We have been able to arrange rupees eighty thousand. The rest we'll be able to scrape together in a day or two.'

'All right. Keep it ready. I'll call in the evening and inform you how and where the money is to be handed over.'

'A word with Maltu...'

'I said this before, haven't I? ...He'll be home once we get the money.'

Yet again they hadn't heard Maltu's voice when the kidnapper had called. Why wouldn't he let them hear the boy's voice even once? This caused a lot of consternation to family members and friends, but there was nothing they could do about it. Some of Devilal's friends and relatives suggested that the police ought to be informed about this development. Others opposed it. After a long-drawn argument that primarily hinged on what would be best for the child's safety, they all decided to not inform the police at that point. Let Maltu return, we can take a call later, was the conclusion.

This is the most critical aspect of kidnapping cases involving ransom calls and threats to kill. Should we or should we not inform the police, the family members keep debating. It is a different matter in case the news has somehow leaked and been reported in the media. Then there is no choice. However, when only family members and close associates know this terrible secret, they want to guard it closely, afraid that informing the police may affect the safety of the kidnapped person.

How can you blame them? It is not about stolen goods, dacoity, snatching that the onus lies with the police to bring the persons to book. When a dear one is being held by some unknown kidnappers and the family members have no inkling as to how dangerous or desperate these persons may be, they prefer to refrain from taking the unnecessary risk of involving the police. Some inform the police once the kidnapped person has returned home after they've paid the ransom.

The Agarwals had the same uncertainties, the same crippling fears. They wanted to be judicious, and they wanted absolutely nothing to go wrong. Any information leaked to the police would put Anurag at risk, so better to not inform them.

It is important to mention here how the police work in kidnapping cases. Officers tend to be just as cautious as family members of the kidnapped persons. Even if someone has the nerves to bring it to the notice of the police, the investigators still have to show prudence. Their job is to get hold of the kidnapper, but certainly not at the cost of an innocent person's life. Let the kidnapped person return, the abductors can be tracked down after that, is their strategy. Attack only if there is a strong backup in place. Tracking down the abductors, retrieving the ransom—all of that can happen later. Therefore, investigators have to prioritise their action, and never take a step if it involves any risk.

After several hours of discussion, the Agarwals decided that Dindayal Upadhyay, Devilal's colleague and friend, would take the ransom money in the Agarwals' car driven by the family's reliable driver Bhawan Sharma. The phone rang at six that evening. The said Mr Gupta instructed Devilal to send the money wrapped in a brown paper tied with red ribbon.

Dindayal set off for Hazra, as directed, following every instruction to the last detail. Middleton Street and Hazra are barely a few kilometres apart. Dindayal was too overwrought to risk being late and therefore ended up reaching earlier than the designated hour. It was 7.10 p.m., ten minutes before he had been asked to be outside Basusree cinema hall. He alighted the car, brown paper packet in hand, rupees eighty thousand in cash inside. It had been tied with a red ribbon as instructed. Then he went inside the car and waited, fingers crossed, his whole mind a prayer, heart pounding against his chest. 7.15 p.m.

His surroundings were filled with people and cacophony as Dindayal waited looking straight ahead with a blank gaze. The shops were filled with groups of people, cars screeched to a halt at the signal then started off again, people were getting back home from work. Hazra crossing was as busy as it always was. At exactly 7.30 p.m., a boy, about ten years old, came and stood outside the car. Dindayal tried to scrutinize the child and observe if there were things he might note for future reference. There was nothing in particular that he would have noticed at first glance. The child was barefoot, with a grubby face, an unclean shirt and a pair of ordinary shorts.

The boy took out a wristwatch from the pocket of his shorts. Dindayal took it and showed it to Bhawan. 'It is Maltu bhaiya's,' he confirmed instantly. Now that there was no doubt that this was the kidnappers' conduit, Dindayal did not waste time—the brown paper packet was handed over to him. The boy took it, and melted into the milling crowd within seconds.

When Dindayal got back to the Middleton Street house, it was 7.45 p.m. The wristwatch set off a storm of cries and sobs in the house—a cruel reminder of the missing boy and that he was indeed in the custody of the monsters. The watch was a Citizen Quartz with a white dial, and it had been Maltu's for sure. Devilal remembered the time he had bought it from New Market for his grandson. Shailendra assured his mother, wife and daughter, and perhaps wanted to renounce his own fears too by saying this aloud, 'The money has been paid. Don't worry, Maltu will be back tomorrow.' As he said this, Shailendra had no clue how hollow and absurd it would sound just a few hours later.

At 9 p.m., the telephone rang at the Agarwals' home. Devilal picked up the receiver. On the other end was the by-now-familiar voice of Mr Gupta.

'What is the matter, Mr Agarwal? Where is the money?' the terse voice from the other end asked. Devilal went stiff with dread.

Somehow, he managed to utter some words with an uncharacteristic arrogance that even surprised himself. 'What do you mean? Upadhyay handed over the packet to a boy. He was given Maltu's wristwatch in turn.'

'We can't find the boy. Don't act smart with us.'

'What are you saying? This is absolutely outrageous. You had promised to release Maltu once you got the money.'

'Yes, if I did. But I got no money.'

Saying this, Mr Gupta hung up on Devilal, who now dropped onto the chair as if all energy had been sapped out of him.

What now? Another round of discussion, careful planning, weighing the pros and cons so that Maltu's safety wasn't put to risk. The Agarwals decided to go to the police this time. There was in fact, no other option. A fresh complaint was lodged with the Park Street police station. Dulal Chakraborty, Sub-inspector in the detective department, was to investigate the case. Chakraborty had handled several complex cases with great success. At the time of his retirement, he was Deputy Commissioner of Police.

The case was a feather in the cap for the Kolkata Police detective department. The Calcutta High Court had observed in the case's verdict: 'The prosecution case as aptly observed by the learned Trial Judge reminds us of a story taken from a thriller.'

It was the end of the 1980s. Those who are now forty years old or thereabouts can evoke enduring vignettes of their childhood days from that time. There weren't thousands of television channels telecasting films, daily soaps, news or sports. One would patiently wait for an entire week for *Chitrahaar*—a half an hour of old and current Hindi film songs. The concluding song would lead to despair as it meant another week's long wait, and some would wonder why there were so many commercials in half an hour and only four or five songs. The following day, children would discuss in school whether that week's *Chitrahaar* had been disappointing or if the concluding song had made it worth the wait.

Hum Log, telecast in 1984, was Indian television's first soap opera made in the Hindi language. The pan-Indian audience lapped it up, making it one of the most popular televisions soaps of all times. Actor Ashok Kumar's brief appearance for a couple of minutes would conclude *Hum Log* for the day. Two years later, the Hindi soap *Buniyaad,* a story woven around Partition was going to be just as popular. Masterji and Lajoji played by actors Alok Nath and Anita Kanwar would captivate Indian audiences for months. They had become part of the Indian family's kitchen and drawing room tête-à-tête. Very soon, the doors would open to a rush of soaps and serials—a majority of them mind numbing and predictably jejune.

A reference to the serials and soaps of the 1980s is

not a digression from Anurag's story. In fact, it is an important context to little Anurag's personality. He was born in 1974 and would be in his mid-40s now had he been alive. Teens and tweens are often drawn to television soaps, but Anurag was totally besotted with the illusory charms of television. He was completely hypnotised by the magic spell of TV—memorising dialogues from soaps and serials, and acting out scenes. Studies and sports were insignificant in comparison. He longed to be a part of that enchanting world, wondering if he could ever make it to the silver screen himself. No one imagined this would turn fatal for the fourteen year old.

Who abducted Anurag? How? The narrative must now travel back to three months prior to the abduction. We have to get introduced to those at the helm of this drama, the makers of this make believe show gone so horribly wrong.

Debashis Banerjee. Age: early thirties. Lived on S.N. Road in Tiljala, east Kolkata. He supplied small-scale orders of various goods from one part of the city to another. His father had long died, and mother got some pension as a 'political sufferer'—a government grant offered to those who participated in the national movement for Independence. Banerjee came from a middle-class family and it was, quite frankly, a hand-to-mouth situation. He was part of a cultural group in south Kolkata's Jadavpur area, where he met Kaberi, a student of Jadavpur University, in 1986. The two fell in love and their marriage was fixed in January 1988.

It took Debashis a great deal of trouble to arrange the money for the wedding. But once the date was finalised, there was hardly any option for its postponement. He took some loans and the amount kept accruing steadily after marriage, to fulfil family demands and expectations regarding social customs and rituals. His brother-in-law worked as a contractor with the Indian Railways and he tried his best to use his contacts to get Debashis some work, but to no avail. The brother-in-law was relatively better off than Debashis, so Debashis took some loans from him, too, but was unable to return the money borrowed. This turned into a huge embarrassment for Kaberi who would often remind her husband that this loan acted as a deterrent to her visits to her parents' home.

Bijon Barua, a resident of Masjidbari Lane in Kasba, also in east Kolkata was a close friend of Debashis. Bijon was a science graduate who offered private tuitions and worked occasionally at a chemist shop. He was a bachelor, and financially as impoverished as Debashis. He too had huge loans to repay.

Debashis and Bijon often discussed the impossibility of escaping from the rut in which they found themselves. Who would offer them money? How would they get out of debt? There would be no stroke of luck. And no, they weren't even criminals that they could hatch a plan for theft, dacoity or snatching.

The impossibility of a practical solution to escape their morbid reality led the duo to give wings to their imagination. As they indulged themselves in these daydreams, their imaginations became more and more audacious. What if they could kidnap someone and demand ransom? This may be the perfect get rich plan, after all!

They even started chalking out the plan in detail. Some pre-conditions were set in the beginning. One, do not target the son of a very rich business family, it could get too risky. It would be leaked to the newspapers, and the police would be after them. The best target would be someone from an affluent family who would be able to pay the ransom money, but not someone absurdly rich. No Tatas or Birlas would do.

Two, no use of force, only tricks.

Three, a hideout was needed. Debashis suggested Bijon's place. Despite his initial inhibitions, Bijon agreed.

Four, some equipment was needed. Debashis bought leucoplast to tie the potential target's mouth and an air purifier mask from Bagri Market. They were novices and therefore mindful that their actions should do no harm to the target. What if an overdose put the target to sleep forever? The idea was to use chloroform in drops so that it seeped into the nostrils. That would be perfectly safe. Bijon got hold of pethidine injection, an analgesic used to relieve pain and chloroform, an anaesthesia that created a drowsy sub-conscious or unconscious condition.

Five, who would look for the potential target? It would be difficult for Bijon to find time for this as he was always running from one place to another, teaching students. Therefore, Debashis decided to take up this part of the work.

For two weeks, Debashis roamed the streets of Kolkata—Esplanade, New Market, Park Street, Ballygunge and Alipore in search of potential targets. Weren't these places inhabited by the rich? He was soon to realize that this was no way to look for a potential target. Even if he made a mental note of someone, it turned out to be impossible to break the ice. After days of such tedious searches and failures, when he was on the verge of giving up, suddenly, out of the blue, Debashis was pleased to see a boy one evening.

It was October 2 and dusk was beginning to descend while Debashis waited for the train to arrive at Esplanade

Metro station. He had got himself a ticket for Jatin Das Park, the Hazra area of south Kolkata. As his eyes were drifting around, he suddenly spotted two thirteen or fourteen year olds engrossed in an animated conversation. They wore clean, smart clothes, and seemed to perfectly fit his criterion. Debashis walked up to the duo and tried to eavesdrop. They were engrossed in discussions on films and TV serials. The train arrived, Debashis followed the teenagers into the train, and took a seat by their side. The boys, unaware of the keen interest the stranger had taken in what they were saying, continued with their conversation.

'Poroborti station Park Street, aagla station Park Street, the next station is Park Street,' the sing-song recorded voice announced, alerting the two boys, who then stood up, ready to leave the train at the coming station. Debashis followed them, though his ride was meant to be till Jatin Das Park, a few stations further.

There, on the Park Street platform, Debashis introduced himself to the teens.

'Excuse me! May I have a word with you?'

'Sure,'

'I am H.K. Gupta. I direct television serials. I would like to discuss something. But, before that, I need to know your names...'

'I am Anurag Agarwal, and this is my friend Samir Patel. What about the serial?'

'Actually, I am directing a TV serial called *Safed Dhagey* meaning white strings. It is the story of a teenager and I have been on the lookout for an actor. But alas, I have yet to meet my lead actor. I saw you on the train and thought you might be perfect for this role. But then, it depends on whether you agree to do it...'

'What are you saying! Of course I am ready to act in it. Who are the other actors?'

Debashis was gleeful that the bait had been taken. Now, onto the careful execution of piercing the hook and picking up the target.

'I'll share all the details. But I need only one boy. Anurag is perfect for this role. Samir, I'll think of a role for you for my next serial. Anurag, will your family agree to this?'

'Of course! But I won't tell them about it in the beginning. I'll surprise them just before the telecast.'

'You know what, there are no fixed schedules for shootings. There may be "call time" any hour of the day. Will your family allow that?'

'I'll manage it, Uncle! When will it be telecast on TV?'

Debashis laughed at Anurag's childishness. He put his hand around the boy's shoulder. The boy had no idea that this man had come to lure him into a fictitious world.

'Don't worry. Let's complete the shoots by the Puja vacation. Better to not share this with anyone at home right now.'

'I won't tell anyone, Uncle!'

Debashis got every relevant detail about Anurag right then. Where he lived, whom he lived with, his telephone number, and promised to call the boy. They even reached an understanding that Debashis would disconnect the line if anyone other than Anurag took the call, reasoning that disclosure at that stage may throw their secret plan out of track. 'Call between ten in the morning to twelve-thirty in the afternoon, and I'll take the call, Uncle!' Anurag gushed with nervous excitement.

That evening, Debashis and Bijon decided they would execute the plan the very next day. On October 3, at around 11 a.m., a call was made to Anurag's home from the Russel Street post office. Post offices during those days had public telephone booths. The boy was asked to reach the Maidan Metro station around 2 p.m. And so he did.

Debashis met him there and informed that it was time for the 'look test'—an indication of how the actor would look on screen. For this, they needed to go to the camera person's place. Debashis took him to Bijon's place, carefully taking a detour, so that Anurag wouldn't be able to locate the place some other time. Anurag was introduced to Bijon as the camera person, Mr Roy.

The story of *Safed Dhagey* was now narrated to Anurag, and 'Mr Roy' took photographs from many angles. But the novice kidnappers were so full of nervous jitters, that despite Anurag walking straight into the trap, they could not pull it off. At 4.45 p.m., Anurag said he was getting late and that his parents would be worried. So Debashis took him to Kalighat Metro and got him a ticket for Maidan.

The next meeting was fixed the following day, for October 4, at Kalighat Metro station, 1 p.m. Anurag was taken to Bijon's place again. But there was a hitch. A neighbour had many people over and there was a lot of noise, and many people were moving around. The plan failed to take off even on that day, and Anurag left after acting out some imaginary scenes out of an imaginary television serial.

Bijon was getting troubled by the boy's repeated visits to his place—it involved great risks as some neighbours may have seen him. Whatever was to be done had to be done quickly now. No more delays, no more risks.

Bijon and Debashis were very serious the third time. They worked on overcoming their nervousness and dread and were sure they would succeed this time around. October 6, 1.30 p.m. when Debashis reached Kasba along with Anurag, Bijon said, 'Today will be your final look test, because shooting starts next week. But your face looks completely sunburnt, how can we shoot? This won't work.'

Anurag was crestfallen. What will happen now?

'Mr Roy, can't we give him an injection to bring back the dazzle on his face?' Debashis inquired innocently.

'Not a bad suggestion. But then, he is likely to feel a bit drowsy though that will be only for an hour or so. When he wakes up, he'll look a lot better and fresh.'

Anurag was now suitably excited at the prospect.

'I am ready for the injection, Uncle.'

So the pethidine injection was given to Anurag with the disposable syringe that Debashis had already bought. But Anurag didn't go into the deep sleep they had expected. He remained awake, only a bit drowsy. After an hour, its effect was gone, and the boy was awake and fully alert. 'Uncle! I think you can shoot now.' The shooting began. It was already evening by then. A neighbour had dropped by to discuss plans for Kali Puja. The kidnap plan didn't materialise even that day. Debashis again left with Anurag to drop him at the Kalighat Metro station. From Rashbehari Avenue crossing, Anurag called up his mother to tell her that he had gone to Alipore Zoo with friends and a punctured tyre in his friend Samir's car had caused the delay. 'I'll reach home in an hour,' he assured her.

'Operation Kidnap' had failed three times in a row. That night, Bijon made it clear to Debashis that they would be wise to avoid his house as a hiding place. Many neighbours had seen the boy and were curious. They must find another place.

So they had to work out an alternative plan. Chalking a plan B isn't always easy, especially when their low confidence and lack of foolproof strategy had led to three failures already. The strategy for the next plan was to increase manpower, because perhaps more brains could make it successful, they thought. Debashis knew someone by the name of Pallab Mukherjee (alias Polu), who lived in Howrah's Bally. He was engaged in part-time brokerage and full-time dadagiri.

Debashis disclosed his plan before Polu the next day. Polu gave him a patient hearing and said, 'All right, there is Ashok Rai, alias Bhoda, from Ghashbagan. You guys come down here on October 11, I would have talked to Bhoda by then. He will find a good hiding place. We'll meet at the Coffee Corner in Howrah station at 11 in the morning.'

On October 11 at Coffee Corner, Debashis and Bijon found Polu and another man. 'This is Gopal Sarkar. He will help us a lot.' The four of them then left for Ghashbagan to meet Bhoda. One dingy lane after another, and turns and bends through bylanes eventually led the four to Bhoda's place. In no time, Debashis and Bijon could tell that Bhoda was a hardened criminal who knew the underworld like the back of his hand. He had a wheat shop near Howrah's Nataraj Hotel—a cover for the mostly various kinds of unscrupulous work he carried out, which gave him power and influence in the area.

The men discussed the most crucial part of the work—distributing the loot, which was, quite naturally, a pre-condition for Bhoda. Next they needed to get down to the important part of reconnoitring the hideout where they could keep the kidnapped child. Bhoda took them to an abandoned, sprawling salt factory, not too far from his place. There were rooms within rooms, one leading to another, criss-crossing the entire length and breadth of the area and labyrinthine passageways. It evoked the Bhul Bhulaiya in Lucknow's Bara Imambara, built more than two centuries back—a place easy to enter, but impossible to find a way out alone.

Bhoda lit a bidi, took a mouthful and said, matter-of-factly, 'This is the best place. Not a soul will know a thing. It's not even guarded at night. You will have to take turns to guard the boy, my men can't do it.'

Bijon and Debashis were not professionals, so they were naturally disconcerted about using such a bizarre place for hiding Anurag. 'How does one guard this haunted place alone at night? Impossible!' Debashis exclaimed. 'Better to find another place.'

Bhoda was a front-foot player, not one to even think of laidback, defensive back-foot strategies. Quickly lighting another bidi, he smiled to indicate that this would not be a problem at all. Within five minutes they had reached another abandoned godown—this one belonging to the Dikshit Transport Company. The company had shut down six months ago, though a guard, Bhagabati, guarded the premises. Bhagabati was into illegal trade of local, spurious liquor, and downed several swigs himself by every afternoon.

Bhagabati handed over the keys to Bhoda without any argument. The storeroom was quite big, stacked with packing boxes of various sizes. Debashis and Bijon thought it just perfect. Yes, this would do.

They went back to Kolkata and got in touch with Anurag the following day. He was asked to meet them at 1.30 p.m. at Kalighat Metro station. It was October 12.

Anurag sneaked out of home without telling his sister or mother, his heart and mind full of dreams to become the next big thing on national television, little realizing he would never return.

Debashis and Bijon first took Anurag to Chandpal Ghat from where they took a launch to cross the River Hooghly to Kolkata's twin city, Howrah. They told Anurag that the shooting location was a particular godown in Howrah district. Gopal, Polu's sidekick whom they had met at the Howrah station coffee shop, was waiting for them on the Howrah side of the ghat. Around 3.30 p.m., he saw them and ran to inform Polu and Bhoda about the long-awaited arrival.

When Bijon and Debashis reached the godown, Gopal stopped them. He took the duo aside and whispered to them: 'No, you can't enter now. Wait till the evening and come back.' So the duo went back to the ghat along with Anurag and waited some more. By then, Anurag was restless. 'My parents will be worried. I've told them I'll be home by evening,' he said. Debashis assured the boy that there were some technical glitches that had led to this inordinate delay. 'Don't worry, we'll drop you home and explain everything to your parents,' Debashis assured him.

Afternoon led to dusk, and dusk soon turned to night by the time the three entered the godown. Polu and Bhoda were waiting inside. Anurag was petrified when he entered the ghostly godown. Where had he come? Where were the cameras, lights, technicians? And who were those two men sitting there in lungis, glasses in hand, smelling foul and with menacing looks in their eyes? There was a packing box in one corner of the godown covered with cloth and a tiny lamp burning in another side of the room. It was eerie and made his blood run cold. The moment Anurag, Bijon and Debashis entered, Bhoda shut the door and locked it from the inside. Bhagabati had just started his liquor business and the low murmurs of his clients could be heard.

Anurag was at his wit's end. He broke down, for the first time realizing that something awful was about to take place. He held Debashis's hand and pleaded, 'Uncle, I want to go home. Please take me away from here. I don't want to act in the serial!'

Debashis and Bijon were both a bit nervous—they could not proceed further in their befuddled state of mind. But Bhoda gauged the situation perfectly. 'He'll now begin to scream. Better to tie him up right away.'

All five of them held Anurag down, stuck the leucoplast on his mouth, and tied up his hands and feet. Then he was made to lie on the packing box, and a few drops of chloroform were dropped into his nostrils through the air purifier mask. The boy turned drowsy, but not unconscious.

Bijon was on guard that night. Debashis left for Kolkata. Bhoda and Polu were to come and check on them from time to time. Debashis returned the next day, on October 13. He learnt from Bijon that the chloroform had been quite ineffective, Anurag had been a bit drowsy initially, but not unconscious. He was tossing and turning all night, Bijon informed.

'Have you called the Agarwals?' he asked, worried.

'Tomorrow,' was the reply.

That night it was Debashis's turn, and Bijon left for Kolkata. In the evening, Debashis, Polu, Bhoda and Gopal were in the godown. Bhoda now began demanding his share. When Debashis informed him that the money had not yet reached him, Bhoda was mad with rage. 'I don't work without advance money. It is only to honour Polu's request that I did this job. I will wait for two to three days... but if I don't get it by then...' He didn't finish the sentence, but the look on his face said it all.

Late into the night, Bhoda took the others to a restaurant. There was masala dosa and kulfi for dinner. When Debashis wanted to pay for the food, Bhoda stopped him: 'No one ever asks for money from me here. I have the last word.' Debashis immediately knew the kind of power Bhoda wielded in the area, and began to worry about how difficult it would be for him to handle this man if the payment got delayed.

Back in the godown, he found Anurag restless and whimpering. His mouth had been tied with leucoplast, so he couldn't make any noise, but tears rolled down his eyes incessantly. Polu noticed it, too. 'It is a bit awkward, the way things are going. This boy studies in an English medium school, lives in Kolkata. Even if we get the ransom, he will spill the beans if we let him go. Now he even knows us by face. We'll get caught and our lives will be finished,' he said, deeply worried.

Bhoda agreed. 'The first to get into trouble will be you, Debashis. It's such trouble working with dolts! Jail sentences don't bother me, I am experienced... I'll be back in months. But you and Bijon will be done for,' he said. Polu agreed. 'Bhoda is right. If this boy stays alive, he will spell doom for us.'

Hearing them, the gullible Debashis became nervous that the plan was going haywire, and worried about the prospect of landing up in jail. Anurag was writhing in pain and discomfort, and Bhoda and Polu were painting a bleak picture of what was to come—it was all so unsettling that he was driven to near madness. 'You are right. There's no point in allowing him to live,' saying this, Debashis leapt and sat on Anurag's chest, putting the full weight of his body on the boy. The others followed. Bhoda wound a gamchha around Anurag's throat while Polu and Gopal held his wiggling feet with their iron grip. Within moments, Anurag's convulsing body went still.

Now what? The boy was dressed in a striped white shirt, maroon trousers and slippers, and wore a gold ring and chain. In his bag he had carried a cream-coloured shirt and a pair of trousers, speculating that an extra set of clothes may come in handy during the shoots. There was also a pair of sunglasses, a camera, a yellow cap, an exercise copy and a pencil. He had trusted the impostors so blindly that he had come fully prepared for every aspect of the shooting, probably even ready to note down the dialogues. He had also carried in his trouser pocket a wallet which contained a neatly placed twenty-rupee note in its folds; there was a strip of vitamin capsules he took regularly following his grandfather's advice.

The men first decided to burn the clothes Anurag had worn. Debashis took out the spare shirt and trousers from the bag. He took these off to Bijon's place the following day. He also later sold Anurag's camera and shared the money with Polu and Bijon. Gopal took the sunglasses and Polu put the medicine strip into his pocket.

Now, onto disposing off the body. The corpse was placed inside a gunny bag, its open end tied with a rope. As the night turned murkier, the four of them left for the ghat on the River Hooghly. They scaled the boundary wall of the salt factory, took turns through dingy labyrinthine lanes and bylanes until they reached the ghat. On the way, Debashis stumbled and cut his foot.

Polu and Gopal slowly entered the dark waters with the heavy gunny bag. They swam for a distance and let it float on its own for sometime, then, allowed its weight to take it down into the depths of the waters until they hoped it had been lost forever.

It was Chaturthi, three days before Durga Puja. But even before the joyful ritual of welcoming goddess Durga into the lives of humans for four days could begin, an innocent boy who had blindly trusted two adults had been thrown into the waters to be washed away forever.

In the court and before the police, Debashis reiterated that there was no prior plan to kill Anurag. A naïve foray into an unknown path, coupled with a debilitating fear of getting caught had led to the murder. And yet, the ruthless manner in which they disposed the body of a young boy shows that some truly dark facet to their personalities was kindled by this event. What they did after put them beyond redemption.

The first phone call was made to the Agarwals on October 14. The bundle of money was handed over to the boy at Hazra the following day, October 15 at 7.30 p.m. Debashis and Bijon had hired a poor boy from the area, explained to him what he was supposed to do (take a packet from the person sitting inside a car and hand him the wristwatch) and paid him a measly five rupees. They collected rupees eighty thousand in cash and divided it into two equal parts. They also devised yet another wicked plan to tell Bhoda, Polu and Gopal that they hadn't been able to extract any ransom at all. But the three hardened criminals from Howrah weren't ones to accept defeat nor cower before a couple of city-bred men trying to fool them. They made serious threats—if the money didn't reach them before Kali Puja which was a couple of weeks away, Debashis and Bijon would face the same consequences as Anurag. No one would ever find their corpses.

The threats made the duo nervous. They decided to call the Agarwals again. The calls started from October 17. By then, the police detective department had started investigating the case. The Agarwals, too, were beginning to sense something amiss.

There were no mobile phones then, else the kidnappers could have been tracked easily through mobile phone towers. Therefore, the Agarwals's landline phone was tapped. Mr Gupta made frequent calls over the next few days demanding the ransom, reiterating that he hadn't received the rupees eighty thousand. But by then, the said Mr Gupta's haughty tone had died down and an urgency and a nervousness was evident in his words. Every time he called, Devilal and Shailendra would ask to hear Anurag's voice, but the same cold reply came: 'The money first.' Neither the police, nor the Agarwals knew at that point that Anurag was no more.

In a few weeks, after a lot of negotiation, the demanded rupees twenty thousand came down to rupees five thousand. The investigators constantly guided the Agarwals and, finally, a trap was laid. Devilal told Mr Gupta he was ready to pay this amount. He was asked to reach Kalighat Temple on November 3, find a particular dustbin and drop the packet containing five thousand rupees inside the bin. The police instructed Shailendra to fill a packet with torn newspapers and drop that inside the dustbin. At 10.15 a.m., a visibly nervous Debashis emerged from a hiding place and surreptitiously moved towards the dustbin. In a blink of an eye, plainclothes police emerged from all around and surrounded him.

'Are you Mr Gupta?'

'No... I mean...'

'Where is Anurag?'

'Anurag who?'

All it required was a slap so powerful it set his head spinning for several minutes.

'Sir, I am Debashis Banerjee. We've killed Anurag. But I wasn't the only one.'

Bijon, Pallab (alias Polu), Bhoda and Gopal were arrested within a few days. The accused admitted to their crime during interrogation.

There was a problem, and a crucial problem. There was no possibility of finding Anurag's body. How could one prove a death in the absence of a corpse?

At this point, the accused were asked if they were ready to submit statements before the court—the exact account and testimony that they had recounted before the police during interrogation. The first to agree to this was Debashis.

There is a major difference between statements made before the police during interrogation and what an accused admits before the court. Under Section 161 of the Code of Criminal Procedure, 1973, the police can record a written account of the statements made by the accused during interrogation. The police officer may 'examine orally any person supposed to be acquainted with the facts and circumstances of the case... the police officer may reduce into writing any statement made to him in the course of an examination under this section.'

However, this statement is not considered as evidence before the court, till the time that this is proven beyond doubt by presenting facts and evidence. Therefore, corroborative evidence is additional evidence, but certainly not independent, self-sufficient proof. That's because there must be a legal protection against the police using force to extract false statements from the accused. Even if a statement has been given to the police under duress, the court gives an accused person the chance to fight it.

The judicial confession (under the Code of Criminal Procedure Section 164), is far more reliable and becomes substantive evidence if it comes voluntarily from the accused. And, if this is further backed up by direct or circumstantial evidence, punishment is certain.

How should the court know if the accused hasn't been forced by the police to give the judicial confession? There are legal provisions for that too. There are certain steps to be followed in the run-up to the judicial confession. First, the police will plead before the court to allow an accused person who is ready for judicial confession to give her/his statement. If this is granted by the court, then the day of confession is finalized. Once the accused arrives in court, there are some specific questions placed before her/him, such as:

Are you ready to give a judicial confession in such and such case? If so, why?

I am a magistrate, I do not belong to the police force. You are not bound by any law to agree to a judicial confession as an accused. But if you do, the statement may be used against you during the trial. Are you aware of that?

Have the police officers told you that you will be released or your punishment reduced if you agree to the judicial confession?

Have you come to give this confessional statement under any kind of duress or pressure? Feel free to say it now.

Has there been any mental or physical torture on you when you were in police custody? If you have any injury marks, you can report it now.

You are under no compulsion to admit to your crime. But if you really wish to, then we give you twenty-four hours' time to think it over again. If you still wish to, only then will your confessional statement be recorded.

There are no police officers here. You are requested to say the truth, voluntarily. If you change your mind, inform us here tomorrow, twenty-four hours later. Whatever you decide will be final.

All of the above questions were placed before Debashis by the magistrate. Debashis did not dither. For once, he was very sure what he wanted to do. When he was asked, 'Why do you want to confess to your crime?' this is what he said, voice quivering:

'My act can never be condoned by those around me. I can have no peace till the time I am punished by law. When the police arrested me and took me home, my mother said she would have much rather preferred to hear about my death. I want to be punished for the crime I have committed.'

Not just Debashis, judicial confessions were made by Gopal and Bhoda as well.

Sub-inspector Dulal Chakraborty, investigating officer in the case, worked hard to pinpoint and collate every bit of evidence, which came across in the lucid narrative of the chargesheet filed in court.

This was indeed a rare case. There have been many cases of abduction and murder in this country. But the Anurag

Agarwal abduction and murder case stands out because the body of the deceased was never found. In official parlance, the 'corpus delicti' meaning the 'body of crime' was absent in the case. This, in plain speak means that there is no evidence that a crime has been committed at all.

Lawyers representing the accused had argued that a person had gone missing, and could not be found, and unless the body is found it is impossible to prove that the missing person had been killed.

There were cases prior to the Anurag Agarwal case, though their number was few and far between, in which murder had been proved in the absence of corpus delicti. Therefore, it was difficult to do so here, but not impossible. The investigating officer's job was as difficult as a mountaineer trying to scale the heights of Mount Everest without an oxygen mask. Yet, Chakraborty knew he could make it.

This meant corroborating every word, every punctuation mark in Debashis, Gopal and Bhoda's judicial confession with circumstantial evidence. The presentation turned out to be top-notch—there were no loopholes, no scope for between-the-line readings.

Every item taken out of Anurag's bag had been retrieved. A number of people had witnessed Debashis and Bijon waiting at the Howrah ghat with a teenager. These witnesses' accounts were collated after showing pictures to jetty employees. When the gang was taking Anurag's body for disposal, they were seen by two garage workers repairing a vehicle under the flickering light of street lamps. Bhoda had threatened them with a caustic 'What are you two looking at, swines? Too clever, huh?' These two garage workers came forward as witnesses.

The godown guard, Bhagabati, turned witness too. He was brought back to Kolkata from his village in Bihar. Bhoda had threatened him with *tu ne bohot kuchh dekh liya, bhaag yahan se, nahi to khallas kar denge* (you've seen a bit too much, leave this place right now, else you'll be bumped off).

Footprints were collected from the godown and though most of them could not be developed into foolproof evidence, some did match with those of Debashis and were accepted as serious clues.

A 'Test Identification Parade' was carried out, where Anurag's friend Samir Patel recognized Debashis as the man who introduced himself as a film and television serial director to him and Anurag at the metro station. Employees of pharmacies from where the pethidine, air purifier mask and leucoplast were purchased were other witnesses.

There were seventy-seven witnesses in all whose statements were painstakingly documented and presented before the City Sessions Court. Finally, the verdict came on 14 December 1991.

All five accused were sentenced with life imprisonment. The case moved to Calcutta High Court. After eleven years of imprisonment, the lower court granted bail to four accused other than Bijon Barua. But this bail was turned down by the High Court and the accused were asked to surrender.

'We are of the considered view that prosecution successfully established a complete chain of circumstances from its oral and documentary evidence which, taken as a whole, unerringly established the guilt of each and every appellant,' the judges wrote.

'I have seen wicked men and fools, a great many of both; and I believe they both get paid in the end; but fools first.' Robert Louis Stevenson wrote in *Kidnapped.*

There may not be a better representation of these lines than in the Anurag Agarwal kidnap and murder case.

The accused were outright evil no doubt, but they were foolish too. Had they been content with the initial eighty thousand rupees ransom and not recklessly demanded more, repeatedly calling the Agarwals, their chances of getting caught would have been zilch.

The investigators may have lost interest in the case due to lack of clues, Anurag's relatives and friends would have blamed their fate for what had come upon them, and the criminals could have roamed free—safe and undisturbed.

Too much guile and greed can bring about such an end for criminals. The wheels of justice keep turning.

THE CLOSET KILLER

The Naolakha murders, 1991

Bhawanipore police station. Case number 563. Date: 25 December 1991. Indian Penal Code Sections 120B, 302, 394, 34: criminal conspiracy, murder, voluntarily causing hurt in committing robbery, acts done by several persons in furtherance of common intention.

Mr Khetawat had been ringing the doorbell of flat 10C for a while now. There had been no reply.

It struck Mr Khetawat as odd. On all other days, Mrs Naolakha would open the door at the first ring at eight-thirty and greet him with a ravishing smile. It was an old habit to have his first cup of morning tea with the Naolakhas. Every single day of the year.

Why were the Naolakhas keeping him waiting today? After a few patient tries, he began to ring the doorbell maniacally, but the door remained shut. He feared they had both fallen ill suddenly. A sudden, unknown fear gripped Mr Jugal Kishore Khetawat.

Most of the Naolakhas's domestic helpers came to work between 8.45 a.m. and 9 a.m. every day. The first one to arrive was Pratima, a reliable hand who even carried with her a set of spare keys to enter the flat in case the Naolakhas were away.

Mr Khetawat was pacing up and down on the landing right outside the door, breathless with apprehension, waiting for Pratima to arrive, unable to stop himself from ringing the doorbell from time to time. Pratima arrived as usual, and after another round of frantic ringing of the doorbell, they decided to use the spare keys.

What they saw inside was a sight as ghastly as it was piteous. The police were informed immediately.

Rameshwar Apartments was a plush eleven-storied apartment complex on Sarat Bose Road, south Kolkata. Flat number 10C on the ninth floor belonged to the Naolakhas.

It was a spacious flat. There was a sprawling drawing-cum-dining area, two bedrooms with attached bathrooms, and kitchen. It was a three-bedroom flat. A part of the drawing and dining space had been separated out as library-cum-study. The flat was stacked with expensive furniture, curios and other knick knacks. But when the neighbour and domestic help entered the flat, they found it in complete disorder—an aftermath of the violence leading to the twin murders.

Fifty-nine-year-old Girish Kumar Naolakha's inert, lifeless body lay on the carpet of the study. He was in a kurta pyjama, an expensive shawl still wound around his neck. Drops of blood appeared to have trickled down from the nose and mouth. There was no doubt that he had been strangulated. A pair of tattered chappals that obviously could not have belonged to Mr Naolakha was lying close to the body. An empty glass was lying around.

Fifty-five-year-old Bina Naolakha's body was in one of the bedrooms, face down in a freefalling posture, a pillow underneath her abdomen. Her nightwear had been ripped brutally, almost torn to shreds. Her face bore signs of scuffles, there were lesions and contusions all over her face, even some bloodshed. One end of a saree had been tied around her neck, the other end attached to the ceiling fan. Her housecoat was in the bathroom, dumped into the commode. The telephone and intercom wires had been snapped.

Girish and Bina Naolakha's son Nilesh and daughter-in-law Anuradha lived with them but had left on a holiday to north India on December 11. They were to return on December 24, but had called a couple of days ago to inform they had not been able to buy air tickets so they would be back on December 26. Nilesh's room was locked, exactly the way it was when they had left.

The rest of the flat was completely wrecked—evidence of either an outburst of anger, malice or a chaotic hunt for something that had been met with stiff resistance. Furniture, curios, utensils, other objects of everyday use lay strewn around. Most of the things from the wooden cupboard in a bedroom were lying outside in disarray, few pieces of wood used to force open locks were lying on the floor. Quite clearly, many valuables had been looted.

It was the morning of Christmas Day. Kolkata has always marked Christmas Eve with great fervour and most people were waking up after a late night to a languid Christmas morning. More celebrations awaited later in the day, but now, buses and people were few and far between, and there was still a lot of time before crowds spilled over at Victoria Memorial, Alipore Zoo, restaurants on Park Street, and various clubs in the city.

The Kolkata Police Commissioner had gone on his morning walk when he got the information about the double murder. He went to Rameshwar Apartments himself right away; the Deputy Commissioner (detective department) was there, and so were officers from the

Bhawanipore police station and the homicide section of the detective department. A flurry of activities started from the time the Lalbazar Control Room had sent an urgent message to all departments concerned: 'Couple found murdered in Sarat Bose Road apartment, reach the spot at the earliest'.

A crowd had gathered outside Rameshwar Apartments by then, and was swelling with every passing moment. It was no easy task to control this group of neighbours and passersby who waited with bated breath to get some more information on the sensational twin murders.

Officers from a local police station usually begin all investigations, but complex cases are generally handed over to the detective department subsequently. On his visit to the scene of crime, the police commissioner decided this case required a probe that could best be handled by the detective department. Sujit Mitra, Sub-inspector of the homicide section was appointed investigating officer in the case.

The probe began. Officers examined almost everything lying around in the Naolakhas' flat. A pair of slippers, glasses, Bina Naolakha's housecoat, chunks of wood from the cupboard... in fact, the entire flat was turned inside out. A 'seizure list' was prepared, hand and footprints in various conditions, quality and sizes were collected. One thing was clear: more than one person was involved in the crime. It would take some more time to figure out who these characters were.

Rameshwar Apartments on 19A, Sarat Bose Road was built by Jugal Kishore Khetawat towards the end of the 1970s. The Khetawat family had dabbled in several businesses though their priority areas were construction and transport. He lived with his family in a duplex flat—10A and 11A—in the building's ninth and tenth floors. On the ground floor, Jugal Kishore and his brother Prahlad had two separate offices, Rameshwar Transport Limited and Bharat Roadways Limited, respectively. Apart from these two offices, the ground floor also had the building's reception, caretaker's office and a community hall. There were four residential flats in each of the floors from the first to the eleventh.

A property in one of the prime locations of the city occupied mostly by the rich business class meant that a number of precautionary measures had been taken for foolproof security. The boundary wall around the building and lawn was reasonably high, sturdy iron gates as high as the boundary wall made it impregnable. One of the two gates was used to enter the premises, the other only to exit. There were two sets of staircases—one for the use of the residents and their guests; the other was for the temporary and permanent domestic workers working in various flats, drivers, milkman, cleaners and newspaper deliverymen. There were two lifts, again along the same differences.

A private security agency—the National Security and Detective Agency was assigned the building's round-the-clock surveillance. Uniformed men worked in three shifts. Every aspect of security was watertight—or so it seemed—uniformed security personnel guarded entrance and exit gates, the basement parking space and the ground floor reception. The reception was connected to every flat through intercom.

The rules were simple. Only faces known to security guards were allowed entry. If these known faces were accompanied by unknown persons, they too were allowed inside. But every individual unknown to security guards had to stop at the reception. After inquiries about names and their purpose of visit, residents were called by the guards through the intercom; only after a go-ahead was received would the guards allow visitors into the flats. Every flat had Yale locks, eye holes on doors, and calling bells.

It seemed that not a chink of light could seep in without the knowledge of the security guards manning Rameshwar Apartments, and yet twin murders had occurred here! Sub-inspector Sujit Mitra tried to imagine how much courage that would require. Or perhaps foolishness, he thought, his face creasing into a wry smile. Not too many—actually no one—had succeeded in making a fool out of the intrepid Mr Mitra. He was not a braggart, in fact, he did not talk more than was required (his piercing eyes did a lot of the work for him). When he was not working, and there weren't too many hours in the day when he could relax, Sujit Mitra probably came across as a shy, nervous man. But he fit well into the role of an investigator. His questions made the persons on the other side of the table jittery. A few words in that rich baritone were enough to make a criminal shake with fear.

It is pertinent to know here that every floor had living quarters for the permanent domestic workers of Rameshwar Apartments—right from the first to the eleventh floor. On the ninth floor there were the Naolakhas in 10C, the Khetawats in 10A, Rajesh Mehta in 10B and Deepak Moghani in 10D. The Naolakhas had three workers who lived on the premises—Pratima (who carried a set of keys with which she had opened the door along with Mr Khetawat to discover the twin murders), and Monika and Shambhu. All of them lived on the ninth floor.

The post mortem report came later in the day. The couple had been smothered and killed. The tentative time of murder: between 10 and 10.30 the previous night.

Clearly, the fortress that was Rameshwar Apartments was not enough to keep away those who wanted to murder for gain. Or was it something else that had led to the couple's murder? Sujit Mitra set off to interrogate the various dramatis personae in this veritable theatre of the macabre. He would note down the dialogues, watch the expressions meticulously—their cries, smirks, laughter, the fear writ on their faces, and try to make sense of them. Would it lead to the inevitable denouement? He would have to follow the riddle on the right path to be able to see it till the end.

It was evident that Girish or Bina Naolakha, one of the residents of flat number 10C had opened the door because s/he knew the person who had rung the bell. Whether it was a resident of Rameshwar Apartments, or one of the domestic workers, it was clear to the police that someone in the building knew and had helped in the loot and murder. *It was an insider job.*

Every resident from each of the thirty-six flats, every temporary and permanent domestic worker and security guard was interrogated. The marathon interrogations continued for the whole of Christmas Day, all through the night and the next day too. No luck. No confession, no disclosure. Obviously, there was one or many perfect liars within the precincts of Rameshwar Apartments, and it was impossible to zero in on them at that stage. Suspicion, without the backing of proof, is mere fluff in investigation.

In the absence of any clear indication as to where the investigations were heading even after forty-eight hours, policemen usually begin to feel under the weather. Sometimes this is influenced by unkind reportage by the media—police failure in a sensational case is always fodder for churning out endless stories. However, the police is no P.C. Sorcar—there is no magic wand in the hands of investigators that can lead to instant unravelling of the mystery.

Technology has helped investigators take major strides. In this case, CCTVs would have helped a great deal, so would electronic surveillance of mobile telephones. The latter gives major leads as soon as a crime comes to light. However, the first mobile phones were introduced in India in 1991—four years after this incident.

But then, in the illustrious history of Kolkata Police, countless cases have been solved with the help of good old, reliable source network. The Eighties and the Nineties contain scores of cases that were solved with the help of the police's source network.

Sources are high-risk high maintenance stuff. A cleverly and judiciously deployed source will reap good results in ninety per cent cases, but neglect and oversight may lead to completely opposite results.

Who are these sources? Obviously, informants that dig out precious gems from the criminal world can't be saints themselves! They would be those nefarious talents that delve deep into the murky world with skilful dexterity, come out unscathed and melt into the outside world as if they were an integral part of it. Lalmohan Babu had told Feluda: I ought to cultivate you. Sources need to be tended to as well. It is one of the greatest skills of a police officer. Not all can do it with aplomb. Those who can, see far more success in cracking a crime. One must be cautious too. It is important to keep checking whether the source is working hard, or whether he has cooked up stories only to keep his job. A spurious source is more dangerous than no source at all. Therefore often, a source needs to be watched by another source. It is thus the police officer's manoeuvring skills with one or more sources through careful plotting and machinations that make the real difference.

Truth be told, the electrifying excitement in Feluda, Byomkesh, Hercule Poirot and Sherlock Holmes crime thrillers is largely absent in actual investigations. Real crime investigations are even ostensibly bland. Rarely do the police come across cigarette butts from incident scenes, foot impressions aren't found on muddy surfaces behind garden weeds, there aren't threat letters or equivalents either. Therefore, if clues are not found from the crime scene or interrogations, the smart police investigator knows he has to dial the number of his reliable source.

Crime thrillers are powerful and dramatic, imaginary sleuths are often smarter than cops. But in real-life crime investigations there in no thrilling excitement in every moment of the investigation—only a lot of hard work, effort and endurance. No imagination running wild, just simple concentration yields results. It involves finding a good clutch of clues and building a case upon it, not creativity.

In this case, too, sources were deployed—not one, but quite a few—each one of them skilful and experienced in their understanding of how the criminal world functions. They were given clear, specific briefings: fill us with inputs on everything the crime world is discussing on the twin murders; has anyone in the neighbourhood—even if unrelated to the crime world—suddenly begun to splurge? Has there been any major change in anyone's lifestyle?

Finally, the much awaited clue was found. The source network hit the bull's eye. It was the night of December 27.

A thek—a form of the superior intellectual adda—near Paddapukur area of Bhawanipore offered the key. The source was a regular in this thek where the main attraction was booze and gambling. Those who frequent these sessions are usually familiar with each other as most of them are inveterate gamblers who have a bittersweet relationship with the city's underbelly. That night, the centre of attraction was a young man splurging on the gambling board with such confidence as if he had always had very deep pockets. He was bragging about his new Yashica Electro 35 camera and he had his own bottle of foreign liquor. His actions were raising a few eyebrows but he was blissfully unaware that he was under intense scrutiny by those around him.

A few pegs down, and the man was belting out an old Geeta Dutt song from the movie *Baazi: tadbir se bigdi hui taqdeer bana le, apne pe bhadosa hai to yeh dnao laga le.*

The hawk-eyed source was neither keen on the song, nor its lyrics. His sixth sense was focused on just one thing—from where had this young man got so much cash? What was his get-quick-rich formula? The smart source casually prepared another peg and offered it to the unknown man. 'Never seen you here before… What work do you do, boss?' The young man was by then too intoxicated to be on his guard. 'I work as a peon in a rich house. But you bet, I am not going to do such dirty work anymore,' he said, casually.

The 'peon working in a rich house' was picked up by the police that night itself. The buzz felt by an intoxicated person disappears the moment they enter the Lalbazar interrogation room. This time there was no exception.

The confession came even before he could be welcomed in. 'Sir, I am Khokon Giri, peon at Mr Khetawat's office. But I have not killed alone. Raju, Kamini and Jagadish were there too, Sir!'

'Right then, tell me how you all did it, and why?'

The reply stunned the interrogators, even if for a brief moment. 'I couldn't resist the money. Madam had offered one lakh rupees.'

'Madam? Which Madam?'

'Vimla Madam. Mr Khetawat's wife.'

Time for the skeletons to tumble out of the cupboard.

The Khetawat and Naolakha families had known each other socially since the Eighties. The Naolakhas then lived in Mullen Street of south Kolkata's Ballygunge area. The ties grew stronger—meals were eaten and celebrations done together. But Vimla Khetawat did not feel comfortable with the newly found family friends. She was withdrawn, introverted, home bound—a conservative woman who was comfortable in her own set-up, family and puja.

The Naolakhas, on the other hand, loved to party, and their favourite haunts were clubs and restaurants. Jugal Kishore Khetawat was a party animal too—parties and the company of like-minded friends were his way of enjoying life.

It was not long before Jugal Kishore Khetawat and Bina Naolakha were drawn to each other. Both were in their mid-forties at the time. In 1986, the Naolakhas moved in to Rameshwar Apartments. His urgency and excitement about having Bina stay close to him led Jugal Kishore to sell the ninth floor flat at a discounted rate to the Naolakhas. Girish and Bina Naolakha both worked in senior positions in private companies and were well-off, but a flat like that in one of the plushest areas of Kolkata was still beyond their reach. Girish could well have guessed why the deal was so attractive, but the reason behind his quiet acceptance and adjustment remains unknown.

Vimla Khetawat differed from Girish on this. No matter how docile she was from the outside, she wasn't willing to adjust to her husband's dalliance (or was it more?) with the confident, attractive neighbour. She left no stone unturned to make her husband come out of the relationship with Mrs Naolakha. The belligerent atmosphere at home didn't change over the years, and there were bitter squabbles. When nothing changed, in her desperation, Vimla took to absurd ways to address the problem. She invited an ojha—a sorcerer to play secret tricks through prayers and chants on her husband so he could come out of Mrs Naolakha's thrall. Nothing worked.

Mr Khetawat would have his first cup of tea and biscuits with the Naolakhas, and spend many evenings at their home playing cards and drinking.

Mrs Naolakha was losing the plot. She began to fall ill. The Khetawats' only son was too wrapped up in himself to interfere with the problems of his parents. Vimla soon found herself fighting this battle all alone.

The lonely, reclusive Vimla was being torn to pieces. Her jealousy turned into bitterness and spite. How long could she lead her life like this? She decided to get rid of the woman who had ruined her life. Not only did she plot Bina's murder, she also thought it best to get rid of Bina's husband. How could he accept his wife's affair? Moreover, it would be easy to get rid of Bina if her husband was killed at the same time; there would be no witnesses.

After the decision had been taken, Vimla plotted its

execution. Obviously, she could not kill them herself. Would Khokon—their reliable peon—agree to do the job?

Khokon had been the Khetawat's company peon for many years. He lived in the office on the first floor, and was sent to Vimla by Jugal Kishore almost every day to his flat with bundles of cash. One day, when Khokon went to the Khetawats' flat, Vimla placed her proposal before him: he would get rupees one lakh in cash—forty thousand as advance payment—for killing Bina and Girish Kumar Naolakha. At first, Khokhon could not believe it. A docile housewife such as Vimla wanting to engage someone to kill two persons! Moreover, Khokhon was only a peon, not a seasoned killer. He turned it down meekly. But Vimla was smart; she knew that such meekness could eventually change and Khokon would fall for the lure of cash. She gave Khokon forty thousand rupees in advance, knowing he would not be able to turn down the idea when he actually saw the money. It worked.

In the 1990s, rupees one lakh meant a lot of money. It was enough for him to quit the thankless job of a peon and start a new business venture. In fact, it was such a huge sum that even if Khokon started a business, he would still have money to spare.

No wonder Khokon agreed, looking at the proposition as a ticket to freedom from a dead-end job. But it was no easy work, and he was realistic enough to figure out that he would require assistance and would have to share the loot if he were to get it done. The lure of cash was difficult to resist, and soon three more persons were part of his team.

Ranjit Rao alias Raju used to work as the Khetawats' driver earlier, but had quit the job and joined a private company as a driver. Soon he came back to Rameshwar

Apartments, this time as driver of Om Prakash Bhuwaniya, resident of flat 7D.

Jagdish Jadav, a cleaner in Mr Khetawat's office was the next one to join the plan. The fourth person was Kamini Kumar Roy, an employee in a south Kolkata garage. Jagdish had introduced him to the others.

The deal was a share of rupees twenty-five thousand each after the job was done, out of which an advance payment of ten thousand rupees each was distributed equally among the four. Khokon and Raju bought expensive Yashica cameras each and Kamini got himself a suitcase.

It was Christmas Eve. Celebrations were on in many flats of Rameshwar Apartment—the clinking of glasses and cutlery, streamers and other decorations, low murmurs of voices, music, dances and laughter. Residents and their guests were coming and going in cars through the gates and the air was filled with whiffs of expensive perfume. The domestic workers too were moving in and out, using either the stairs or the lift. Khokon and his gang decided to strike then—the busy evening would be ideal to get the job done.

Moreover, Vimla was herself keeping a track of the entire proceedings. She had taken her role of the kingpin very seriously. She knew Bina and Girish's son and daughter-in-law were away and would return on December 26, and had informed Khokon accordingly.

Khokon, Raju and Jagdish were all known to the security guards. Only Kamini was an outsider. Since known persons were allowed to take guests along, Raju took Kamini to his living quarters on the sixth floor around nine in the evening. The guards did not stop them. Jagdish went in a little later, and joined them.

Vimla Khetawat rang the Naolakhas's doorbell at exactly 9.30 p.m. Bina opened the door. A courteous Vimla told her that her husband had possibly left behind his container of Pan Parag in their flat. Could she look for it? 'He can't find it. He comes here so often and is careless at times. Could you look for it, please?' Vimla delivered the lines with an underlying sarcasm. Looking at Bina, the smart, extroverted woman who loved partying and was in love with her husband, Vimla felt a thrill she had never felt before. Standing near the door, watching her now looking for a Pan Parag container with awkward nervousness, Vimla felt powerful and liberated. The poor lover of her husband didn't know she had less than a few hours to live. Standing there, Vimla made sure that the Naolakhas' staff had left for the day.

Khokon was waiting near the intercom to hear from the boss. The phone rang exactly at 10 p.m., as decided earlier. Vimla gave the green signal. The line was clear and the time had come to strike. Jugal Kishore had by then gone to bed, their son Anil had left for a party, he would be late.

Khokon took the stairs and went to the sixth floor where Raju, Jagdish and Kamini were waiting for him. They were armed with an iron blade and a spade which they put inside a large bag.

The doorbell at the Naolakhas's 10C flat rang again at 10.05 p.m. Seeing Khokon's familiar face through the eyehole, Girish Naolakha opened the door casually. Khokon and the other three pounced on him without giving him any time to react. Girish tried his best to fight back but it was a battle that he had lost even before it had begun—three young men had caught him unawares. He was wearing a kurta-pyjama with a shawl wrapped around. Khokon caught the shawl's free end, wound it around Girish's neck and pulled hard twisting his neck between the two ends. They threw him down on the floor, but the scuffle did not last for more than a few minutes.

Bina was in the bedroom when the bell rang. She heard noises from the hall and came out rushing. In her desperation to save herself from the four assailants she made a dash for the telephone in the drawing-cum-dining space. But the intruders had already snapped all lines. Bina was brutally assaulted, and a sari was picked up from the bedroom and wound around her neck. Its other end was tied to the bedroom ceiling fan. She tried to resist, screamed for help, and possibly due to this, a pillow was quickly pressed against her face with full force to smother her.

After the Naolakhas had been killed, Khokon and the others broke open the guest room cupboard and filled their bag with all that they could lay their hands on. Happy with the way their plan had succeeded, they sneaked out through the main door and clicked it shut from outside, ensuring they hadn't been seen by anyone.

Khokon, Raju and Jagdish went back to their respective living quarters, took leisurely baths and hit the bed. Kamini was the only outsider. He had to make sure he woke up at the crack of dawn, scaled the building's high boundary wall and slipped out furtively with the looted goods. It was easy to guess that the security guards would be tired and groggy at that hour, their eyes heavy with sleep, so it would be easy to quietly slip out. The plan was to share the loot equally at an appropriate time.

Once Khokon made his statement, Vimla Khetawat was arrested. She admitted to her crime almost immediately. She was morose, nonplussed and icy cold at the same time, as if she had taken the extreme step with the knowledge that it could not be kept under wraps for too long. And yet she had chosen to go down that terrible path. Raju and Kamini were also soon in the police net. Jagdish had fled to his native home—a remote village in Bihar, from where the investigating team picked him up soon. The four had distributed the stolen goods amongst themselves on the night following the twin murder.

A large amount of jewellery, watches, expensive curios was retrieved, all of which were identified by the Naolakhas's son and daughter-in-law.

It's always tough to understand a criminal mind and see the whole picture by bringing together different parts of a jigsaw puzzle. Khokon, Raju and Jagdish were all employed in the building and knew that fleeing the scene of crime would raise suspicion, so they deliberately stayed on in the building. It wouldn't have been wise to quit their jobs the day after the murders. And yet, it is baffling how they had managed to go about their daily work as usual, without giving the slightest hint. They were neither tense nor edgy, and had answered every query matter-of-factly during police interrogation, and served tea to the officers of the investigating team. In a nutshell, they had nerves of steel and had managed to bluff the police.

Sujit Mitra, the investigating officer, could make criminals nervous with his questions but it didn't work in this case. That's what makes every case a new learning experience for the sleuths, there are so many different means to the end. The criminals had put on the masks of simple domestic workers and the kingpin was an ordinary housewife with a cool demeanour throughout the interrogation. But something else had clicked for Sujit in this case: his brilliant source network. Sujit worked as officer-in-charge of the homicide section for many years and retired a couple of years ago as Deputy Commissioner, special branch.

In crime thrillers, the police officer's job ends when a nervous criminal is drubbed by the sharp arguments of the private detective as the nervous police officer looks on. He faces crushing humiliation in the hands of the handsome detective, and puts the handcuffs to good use in the end—his only real contribution to the story.

In real-life crime cases, however, the police officer must work hard not just to get hold of the criminal, but also to file the chargesheet and ensure the arrested gets punished in the court of law. If he fails in this part of the job, the arrested will easily slip away. And then nothing can be achieved in retrospect.

Sujit Mitra now concentrated on the second part of the job. Khokon and Raju had bought expensive Yashica Electro 35 cameras from Garfa Main Road. The cash memos were procured from this shop. Kamini had bought a suitcase with the advance payment from a Bhawanipore store. This cash memo was collected as well. Kamini had a cut mark on his right foot—an injury from the sharp edge of the pointed ends along the boundary wall, which he had scaled while escaping around dawn. There were bloodstains on the boundary wall, which was medically tested to prove it was Kamini's blood. Several hand and footprints from the crime scene were collected and sent for forensic tests, and some of them matched with those of the attackers. Moreover, Khokon and Raju had submitted judicial confessions before the court.

Presenting a foolproof case before the court after

arresting the culprits even if they have admitted to the deed during police interrogation is still a tough job. In complex cases such as this, the investigating officer must string together evidence against the accused, arranging them in the order of the sequence of events.

The trial began after the Kolkata Police filed their chargesheet within three months, armed with investigative findings, medical reports and other evidence. One of the accused, Raju, became a state witness, making the police's job easier.

The Khetawat family was affluent and they used the money and power at their disposal to hire renowned lawyers who were stars in their field. Public prosecutor Sisir Ghosh, an experienced professional fought the case for the Kolkata Police. There was despondency and cheer for both parties at various stages of the court proceedings.

In 1991 the Alipore district and sessions court ordered life imprisonment for Vimla Khetawat, Khokon Giri, Kamini Kumar Roy and Jagdish Jadav. Raju, who had turned state witness and had helped fill in the critical gaps of the narrative and supplied adequate proof to help build a strong case, was released on the basis of the prosecution plea.

The case moved to the Calcutta High Court, where the Kolkata Police fought the case against another group of renowned lawyers who were defending the Khetawat lady. In 2006, the High Court gave the same verdict as the lower court.

The next step was the Supreme Court of India. By then, Vimla Khetawat was seriously ill. One side of her body was paralysed, and many other ailments had crippled her mind and body. This led the Supreme Court to grant her bail, on the condition that she would surrender once her health improved. Vimla went back to the Sarat Bose Road flat.

The Supreme Court of India's verdict was the same. But by then, Vimla Khetawat had freed herself from all worldly attachments. On a sultry June afternoon in 2008, she jumped to her death from the balcony of her Sarat Bose Road flat. The crutch which she used to support herself was found lying by her side.

Why did Vimla kill herself? Was she afraid of going back to jail? Was it social humiliation or just plain guilt? Perhaps this was the only conclusion possible for a life that had shrivelled into nothingness.

A CURIOUS PLACE TO HIDE

The Biswanath Dutta murder case, 1994

Burtolla police station. Case number 62/94. Date: 6 March 1994. Indian Penal Code Sections 120B, 302 and 201: criminal conspiracy, murder and causing disappearance of evidence or giving false information to screen offender.

'Don't you read newspaper inserts? Really? What do you read then?' Byomkesh raised his eyebrows and asked, with genuine curiosity.

'I read what others read in newspapers—news!'

'Ah! About bloodshed in Manchuria caused by severed fingers, birth of triplets in Brazil, that's what you read. What good is that? If you want real news, read newspaper inserts.'

I couldn't let go of this opportunity for a bit of needling. 'Of course! The newspaper guys are such devils! Instead of filling up entire newspapers with inserts, they waste pages publishing useless news.'

Byomkesh's sharp eyes lit up suddenly. He said, 'No point blaming them. They can't sell their papers unless they pander to entertaining people like you. But the real news can be found in inserts. Whatever happens around the country, whosoever hatches crafty plans for looting people in broad daylight, all those secret ploys to pack off looted goods—if you want such important news, you must read the inserts. The Reuters telegrams won't have that stuff.'

The telephone at Burtolla police station rang at 4.45 in the morning.

'There's a lot of trouble going on here, Sir. Please come down.'

'What do you mean by here?'

'2C Beadon Street. The swine has murdered someone, Sir!'

'Murder?'

The duty officer disconnected the line. Just fifteen minutes into the morning duty and news of murder from the first call received! If morning shows the day, well, this was it! He knew what his day was going to be like.

The address given by the caller was barely a kilometre from the Burtolla police station. When the police jeep sped from the thana and stopped outside the given address, a disorderly group of nearly three hundred people had already gathered around the house even at that early hour. Shrieks and screams—neighbours, or perhaps some tenants and residents of the house—made it difficult to figure out what exactly had happened. Their angry pitch increased several notches on seeing the policemen. 'We'll hang the cur to death, Sir! You all can go back,' the crowd yelled at the men in uniform.

Investigating the murder now took a back seat. First, the law and order situation had to be addressed. It was a narrow, congested area, and it was filled with a group of inquisitive, angry people, their numbers rising by the minute. The officer quickly sent a wireless message to the police station. From there it reached Lalbazar. *Commotion at Beadon Street over suspected murder. Reinforcement required as early as possible. Please inform superiors.*

Lalbazar informed the Deputy Commissioner

(North Division) and Deputy Commissioner (detective department). The OC rushed, as did the officers from Lalbazar's homicide section. The police stations surrounding Burtolla sent forces to Beadon Street. The Control Room informed the officers: 'DC North and DC-DD on the way. Situation report every five minutes, please.'

31 January 1994, Monday. Abhijit Dutta was poring over the classified advertisement columns of *Anandabazar Patrika* in his Chandannagar home. He was looking for a job and therefore read every advertisement under the 'Jobs' columns and made notes on where he wanted to apply. Suddenly, a particular insert under the 'Land/Houses for Sale' column caught his eye. His eyes popped out in disbelief.

NOTICE

The Premises at 2C Beadon Street, Calcutta 6 under Bartala P.S. within Calcutta Municipal Corporation will be sold. If there are any sharers or claimants other than the two sharers of the premises at the said address, he should contact within seven days of publication of the said notice at the following address.

Bikash Pal, Advocate, Small Causes court.
2/1 Kiran Sankar Roy Road, Calcutta 1

Not once, Abhijit read it twice. Then he dashed to the next room where his father was sitting, and asked him nervously, 'Baba! Have you seen this?'

It was 9.15 in the morning. Amarnath Dutta was preparing to leave for work after breakfast. He was a bit surprised to see his son worked up. The boy had a calm disposition; expressions of anxiety were simply against his nature.

He took the newspaper from his son. 'What's the matter? What's there in the newspaper? Let me see...'

Amarnath read it and understood the reason his son was so flustered. He would leave for work a little later today. He dialled a number in Kolkata from the drawing room landline phone.

'Samar, have you read today's *Anandabazar*? Page 2, advertisements, "Land/Houses for Sale" column...'

Jagannath Dutta had built a three-storeyed house on Beadon Street in the Seventies. He passed away in the early Nineties, and his wife died three years later leaving the Beadon Street property to their four sons and a daughter.

The eldest, Amarnath, was a bank officer who lived in Chandannagar with his homemaker wife and son Abhijit, who was pursuing higher studies and on the lookout for a job.

Second son Samarnath, worked and lived in Kolkata, though not in the Beadon Street house.

The third, Biswanath, a bachelor, worked at the Dharmatolla branch of the United Bank of India. He had two obsessive interests—music, and numismatics, i.e., collecting old coins. Biswanath spent more than half his salary buying records and cassettes, remained confined to his two rooms on the second floor of the Beadon Street house, and needless to say, had made no enemies.

The youngest brother Aloknath was a Kolkata Police constable. He lived on the first floor of the Beadon Street house, occupying two rooms and a covered balcony with his wife Mamata, a son and two daughters. Aloknath's brother-in-law, Shibshankar, aka Babu who was without a job, lived in the covered balcony area that was used as a bedroom.

Their sister Anuradha lived with her husband and in-laws in Kolkata's Fakir Chakraborty Lane.

The ground floor rooms were given out on rent, and the earning from this was divided equally among the siblings. Rooms on the first and second floors which belonged to Amarnath, Samarnath and Anuradha were left vacant and unused, and were meant for their use whenever they visited.

It would have been foolish to waste time after such a newspaper insert came to their knowledge. Amarnath immediately got in touch with Samarnath and Anuradha. They drafted a joint letter stating that they were co-owners of the Beadon Street house and therefore, selling it without their permission was illegal. In the second week of February, they sent this letter to the lawyer whose name was published in the insert.

The obvious question would be: why did they not discuss the matter with their brothers Biswanath and Aloknath? It is important here to note the dynamics of the relationship between the siblings.

Biswanath led a very ordinary life, was reluctant about social interactions, and unwilling to discuss money or property matters. Aloknath was poles apart. He was drawn to worldly pleasures, more at home in horse race betting and gambling, a heavy drinker and a familiar face in prostitutes' quarters.

Biswanath, who lived in the same house as Aloknath,

never intervened in his brother's affairs. But Amarnath, Samarnath and Anuradha had a bitter relationship with their youngest brother; they were totally against his wild and undisciplined lifestyle. They weren't even on talking terms, and the three of them hadn't stepped into the house since their parents' death.

On seeing the newspaper insert, they felt Aloknath had somehow tricked the simple Biswanath into a plan to sell off the house. But now that it had come to their notice, they felt greatly relieved that the letter of objection had been sent to the lawyer. The devious plan would be nipped in the bud.

Samarnath had to travel outside Kolkata on work, and was scheduled to return in the last week of February, therefore Amarnath decided that the two of them would visit Beadon Street in the first week of March after Samarnath's return.

The matter required urgent attention. What was he thinking when Alok decided to sell off the house without their knowledge? Some sense needed to be driven into Dhabu's head too (Dhabu was Biswanath's pet name). How could he get tricked into it and inform no one? He had never been greedy for money. What was it then?

The answer was revealed on the morning of March 6.

The day before, Amarnath and his son Abhijit had reached Samarnath's Kolkata home. They planned to go to Beadon Street from there at around 2 to 2.30 a.m.

There was a reason behind choosing to visit Aloknath at that rather odd hour. If Alok was on morning shift, he would leave home by 5 a.m., and they may not see him if they went in the morning. Knowing him, he would leave for work to avoid discussion and not return for a couple of days. Better to catch him when he was sleeping.

When they reached the Beadon Street house and knocked, Alok opened the door half asleep, and was startled to see his brothers.

'You?'

'We haven't come down for days, thought we'd find out how things are going. Upstairs, we found Dhabu's room locked from inside. When we knocked someone spoke in Hindi asking us to come back later. Where's Dhabu?'

'Oho! Forgot to tell you, Dhabu-da moved to Barasat fifteen days ago. He took a rented accommodation there.'

'What! But why Barasat?'

'He said he'll be transferred to the Barasat branch soon. It would be difficult to travel daily from here. So he got an accommodation...'

Amarnath stopped him midway through the tall tales. His brothers could see through the lies.

'Stop all this nonsense. Tell us what happened. Why are our doors locked from the inside? They always remain open! Where's Dhabu?'

'Told you he moved to Barasat. If you don't believe me, go visit him. 11/1 Jhowtolla Lane, near Barasat Chowrasta. Why are you screaming at me?'

'You know why we are so upset! Why are our rooms shut? Where's Dhabu? Who's inside Dhabu's room? What have you done? Let's come back from Barasat and we'll see this through to the end!'

All that noise in the middle of the night had an effect that eventually came to good use for the visiting brothers. The high drama woke the ground floor tenants, as well as the family living on the first and second floors. They came to inquire what the hollering in the dead of night was all about. When Somnath inquired who they were, a middle-aged man came up to introduce himself: '*Mera naam Nandlal Singh. Alok-babu aur Biswanath-babu apna apna hissa mujhe bech diye thode din pehle.*' (My name is Nandlal Singh. Alok-babu and Biswanath-babu sold off their respective shares to me some days ago).

'What? *We* are the owners of those rooms! What do you mean you purchased them?'

'Ask Alok-babu! I've got an agreement, you can see it.'

When Nandlal rushed to get the agreement, Samarnath grabbed his younger brother by the collar of his shirt. Aloknath was quite clearly on a sticky wicket, unable to utter a word. His wife Mamata too was mum with dread. Amarnath stopped his brother, Samarnath, asking him to show some patience and restraint.

'Let's go to Barasat first. What could have happened to Dhabu! Let's find out first, then we can come back and settle this.'

Amarnath, Samarnath and Abhijit stepped out of the Beadon Street house and immediately took a taxi for Barasat.

It was 4.15 in the morning when they returned. They had located the address in Barasat, but some other family lived there, not their Biswanath. Their worst fears had come true. Aloknath had told them an out and out lie.

Their patience had run out by then. Amarnath and Samarnath could no longer show any more self control or leniency towards their youngest brother. They rained slaps and blows on Aloknath, along with furious, anxious demands to be told the truth this time, 'Tell us what you did! Else, we'll kill you.' The tenants too supported the two brothers, demanding to know from Aloknath where Biswanath was.

Beaten black and blue, Alok could not take the assault for more than five minutes. He gave in.

'I've buried him.'

'What?'

~

After the arrival of additional force, the policemen were finally able to enter the premises of 2C Beadon Street. Aloknath was crouched on the first-floor balcony, his bent head resting on folded knees, submerged in silence. Mamata stood in a corner, head hung, eyes lowered. A number of tenants were in the covered balcony area, while Amarnath stood there, looking disconsolate. Samarnath was completely exhausted, wiping tears from time to time. Abhijit tried his best to console his uncle.

Amarnath came running as soon as the OC entered the room. 'Come, Boro-babu! I am Amarnath Dutta.'

'What's the matter? Heard about a murder...'

Samarnath burst out crying. He ran towards Aloknath and gave him a vigorous shake on the shoulders.

'Sir, he is the one! He! He has killed Dhabu and buried him. He has killed his own brother, prepared fake documents and sold off the house. He has brought shame on his family. Hang him, Sir...'

The officers understood how difficult it would be for them to work in such an emotionally charged set-up. The interrogation had to be done privately. A raging, furious mob was controlled with difficulty as Aloknath was taken to Burtolla police station.

'Tell us everything. You work with Kolkata Police. You know the rules, so you know the earlier you disclose everything the better it is for you. The more you delay, the more damage you bring upon yourself, hope you don't need to be told that?'

Over the last few hours, Aloknath had been severely beaten up by his brothers. His lips were swollen up, his hair dishevelled, he was breathing irregularly. Finally he got talking. He began to narrate the chain of events, slowly lifting the curtain to reveal a deep, dark secret.

~

What would have been the salary of a constable twenty-five years ago? Whatever the amount, it was certainly not enough to lead an uncontrolled and extravagant life and run a family at the same time. Aloknath was unable to exercise control when it came to races, gambling, drinking and women and the pressure of unpaid loans was consuming him bit by bit. He started to look for a way out of the desperate situation.

There was only one way out. If the first and second floor of the house were sold off, it would bring in a lot of money. But would Bor-da, Mej-da and Didi agree? The chances were nil. What about Dhabu-da? He wanted to give it a try. He placed the proposal before Biswanath in November of 1993, and was totally crestfallen by his reaction.

'Why should we sell off the house? We are doing fine!'

Perhaps Biswanath was doing fine, but not a debt-ridden Aloknath. No, he wasn't doing well at all.

And thus was sown the seeds of a plan to bump off the simpleton brother. A conduit was ready at hand—his unemployed brother-in-law Shibshankar. His wife Mamata too played an important role in scripting the murder. Shibshankar's brother-in-law, Mrinal Dutta also joined them. An ordinary bank employee, Mrinal lived in Nimta of North 24 Parganas district, adjoining Kolkata, and was a regular at the Beadon Street house.

Aloknath—pale and haggard from the interrogation—broke into a disjointed narrative from time to time as he burst into tears, 'What have I done! Forgive me, Sir.' The sleuths were quite familiar with such reactions, and they too kept harping on just one thing—'So, what happened next?'

'I got in touch with some brokers. They got some buyers pretty quickly too. Shibshankar, my brother-in-law, my wife and I approached Mrinal to join us in executing the plan. We asked him to sign the legal documents as Biswanath Dutta. He wasn't ready initially, but we offered him some money. Mrinal earned a paltry salary, so he eventually agreed.'

'Then?'

'Then the deal was finalized with Nandlal Singh. Nandlal came down to take a look at the house. We showed him around when Dhabu-da was at work, and introduced Mrinal as Biswanath Dutta and Mamata as my sister. The agreement was to sell the rooms of the first and second floors. It was signed in mid-January by Mrinal and Mamata as Biswanath and Anuradha respectively. I got approximately 60,000 rupees in advance.

'Nandlal was in a hurry, he wanted immediate possession. The remaining payment was to be made only after he entered the house and the property was registered in his name. But how could he move in as long as Dhabu-da was there? After all I had taken the advance, and we had already rented a flat at Ashwini Nagar in Baguiati where we were supposed to shift after the house was sold off.'

'Then...?'

'Sir, there was no other way but to finish off Dhabu-da.'

'How did you do it?'

'On January 22, Dhabu-da returned home at around 10.30 p.m. I asked him to sleep in our balcony area saying masons had been working on some repairs. He was an uncomplicated person and never doubted me. Around 12.30 a.m., Shibshankar, Mrinal and I covered him with a blanket and throttled him. The following day, I asked Nandlal to take possession of the rooms. They came down, and I pleaded with him to give me another day as it would take time for me to move out with such a huge number of belongings. He agreed.'

'Where's the body?'

'Buried it, Sir.'

'I got that. But where have you buried it?'

Alok was silent. A shake by the collar and he muttered.

'Near Nimtala Ghat, Sir.'

'Can you show us the place?'

'Yes, Sir.'

A vehicle rushed towards Nimtala Ghat without a moment's delay. Alok showed a place, then directed the car onto some other area as if he had suddenly lost the way.

Investigators are familiar with such bouts of memory losses in people being interrogated. They understood that he was not going to disclose the place quite so easily. All it required was a visit to Lalbazar. At the police station he wasn't ready to give in to threats nor was he afraid of the impending punishment but the police headquarters were a different matter altogether.

But first, Aloknath and Biswanath's rooms were to be searched thoroughly. The morning's madness hadn't left scope for this essential aspect of the probe. Then, on to Lalbazar. It was not going to be easy for Aloknath to guard his secret close to his heart for too long, the officers were confident about that.

The Beadon Street house again. By then, the detective department sleuths had taken over the entire house.

They were preparing a map of the house. Shibshankar and Mamata were being interrogated, though they hadn't yet spilled the beans. A police team was en route to Mrinal's Nimta house to get him. Another group was preparing a list of persons to be interrogated immediately and the entire flurry of activities was being supervised by the DC-DD and DC-North.

Atanu Bandopadhyay, a twenty-eight-year-old Sub-inspector (now Assistant Commissioner in the detective department), was part of the homicide team. He was a favourite of his seniors on account of his sharp mind, alertness and a great hunger for unearthing mysteries.

Atanu was walking placidly among his colleagues who were busy looking out for clues and compiling important facts. It seemed Atanu was pottering around the house, but no one knew that he was actually in deep thought and that the result was going to be a stunning discovery.

The officers were sniffing around for clues here and there, preparing the seizure list, forensic experts were looking for hand and footprints in the balcony and the rooms, Mamata and Shibshankar were about to be taken to Lalbazar, when something on the wall of Nandlal's room caught Atanu's eyes.

Nearly every room in the house had an elevated structure to place idols for worship. Didn't the one in this room appear slightly different from the others? Didn't the construction look somewhat freshly done? The walls in the room were white, only this elevated portion was a pale peach in colour. Like the flash of a sudden lightning a brainwave struck.

'Sir, could you come here?'

The DC-DD and others walked up to where Atanu stood examining the portion of the wall. Yes, they all agreed. This looked somewhat different from the other rooms. Aloknath was quickly brought there. In no time he was ready to disclose the secret.

'I buried Dhabu-da here, Sir!'

Aloknath had killed his brother, concealed the corpse behind a wall in the house and had sold off the property! What a devious plan! The experienced officers were stupefied by the savagery of the act. Masons were immediately called in, and as the first sharp edge of a metal blade was rammed into the concrete, a putrescent odour filled the room. They looked on as the freshly constructed part of the wall was brought down, open-mouthed at the nerve of a man who could do this and still remain stable for so long.

The corpse was taken out a month and a half after the murder. It was more of a skeleton, with some decomposing, maggot eaten flesh clinging onto bones around the neck, throat and chest.

Finally, at the interrogation table, Aloknath disclosed how he had killed his brother Biswanath.

22 January 1994. Biswanath had returned home at 10.30 p.m. after watching a cultural show organized by his office at the Khudiram Anushilan Kendra, in central Kolkata. He had bumped into Aloknath as he was about to take the stairs to reach his room.

'Dada, could you sleep in the balcony adjoining my room tonight?'

'Why? What's the matter?'

'I've engaged some masons to do some repair work. The rooms are in such a mess. Just forgot to inform you earlier. They are doing the second floor today, tomorrow and day after it will be the first floor.'

Biswanath could see some cement filled bags on the staircase between the first and second floors. He trusted his brother completely.

After dinner, he went to sleep in the covered balcony area adjoining one of his brother's rooms—relaxed and peaceful. Mrinal had reached the Beadon Street house by 9 p.m. as planned, waiting in Aloknath's other room. Shibshankar was skulking around, patiently waiting for the prey. By 11 p.m., Aloknath's children were fast asleep in the adjoining room.

When the clock struck 12.30 a.m., Alok stepped out of his room and returned within five minutes.

'Dada is fast asleep. Mamata, give me the blanket.'

Shibshankar, Mrinal and Alok took the blanket and went to the thin strip of balcony where Biswanath was sleeping soundly. Shibshankar tiptoed in, held Biswanath's feet together with his firm grip, while Mrinal caught his hands. Alok lunged for his brother's head. He put the blanket on his face and pressed as hard as he could. He was at it for a good seven minutes or so. Biswanath's desperate struggle was evident from his wiggling feet and flailing arms, but all of it stopped after a few minutes. When he was sure his brother would have breathed his last, Aloknath removed the blanket and took his hand near the nostrils to examine Biswanath. The man wasn't breathing. He shut the eyes that were staring at him…

…The work was done.

But more work was left, eventually completed by Alok,

Mamata, Mrinal and Shibshankar together. Only a few days earlier, Alok had engaged masons to construct a supporting base for an elevated space to keep idols for worship in the same pattern as in the other rooms. Therefore cement and sand were ready at hand.

Biswanath's body was placed inside the vacant space with the legs folded, and the remaining part of the elevated portion of the wall was covered with bricks and cement painstakingly till the morning's wee hours. Mrinal left, Shibshankar went off to sleep in the balcony as usual in exactly the same place where Biswanath had been murdered just a few hours ago. Aloknath and Mamata went off to sleep too, unrepentant and unperturbed that the body lay buried in another room of the same house.

Atanu Bandopadhyay headed the probe team. Such an incident naturally sent shockwaves through the entire city. Imagine a policeman killing his own brother and burying the body behind the wall of a house where he continued to live!

Naturally, there was pressure to file the chargesheet quickly so the guilty could be punished as early as possible. Aloknath's nature was indication enough for the sleuths that he was likely to disown his statement in court. Therefore, the circumstantial evidence had to be very strong.

Alok, Mamata and Shibshankar were arrested the day the corpse was found. Mrinal was arrested from his Nimta home the next day.

Investigation is a marathon race. Arresting the accused is just the first ten out of the forty-two kilometres the runner is required to cover. The remaining thirty-two kilometres involve submitting the chargesheet in court along with collecting evidence, and the court granting punishment for the accused. Atanu had just started the warm up of his marathon race.

Three trunks belonging to Biswanath were found from the flat rented by Alok (where they were to shift soon). These contained his clothes, a large number of old coins, music cassettes and records he had lovingly collected over the years.

There was more shock in store, more proof of how low Alok could stoop for money. A pump set and some utensils belonging to Biswanath was found from the house of one Gobindo Sardar, resident of 24/A Nimtala Ghat Street. Sardar admitted that Alok had sold these to him.

Mrinal, Mamata and Alok had signed the documents on the property sale. Their specimen handwriting was collected and sent for forensic tests, and there were no surprises in the result.

Alok worked in the Armoury section of the Police Training School. The attendance register showed that he had joined duty on January 23, but left early under the pretext of his daughter's illness and joined work after a week. During those seven days, he was transferring the property to Nandlal and removing all possible evidence of the murder.

In mid-January, Aloknath had purchased cement and sand from the shop of a person called Soumitra Nayak. The shop and its owner were both located.

Mrinal Dutta meanwhile, agreed to a judicial confession, in which he described every detail of the murder.

Lawyer Bikash Pal's statement, too, was extremely relevant to the case—he was the one who had placed the insert in *Anandabazar Patrika*.

During the property transfer, Alok had claimed that he had two brothers and a sister, though the municipality records showed he had three brothers and a sister. Alok repeatedly evaded questions or denied it when asked to explain. In order to clear his doubts, Bikash had resorted to a newspaper insert (he had been engaged by Nandlal to probe whether the property was disputed) that had acted as the main catalyst in unravelling the murder.

The main work was still left: proving beyond doubt that the near-skeletal remains actually belonged to Biswanath.

Dr Apurbo Kumar Nandy, head of the Forensic and State Medicine department of Calcutta Medical College and Hospital did the post mortem. Dr Nandy, who had conducted several thousands of post mortems, wrote in his report: 'Death in my opinion was caused by compression of neck, for example, throttling ante-mortem and homicidal in nature.' The age of the deceased was mentioned as approximately forty-three. Amarnath, Samarnath and Anuradha informed the police that Biswanath had a buck tooth and the post mortem report had a special mention of a buck tooth. This, in fact, was considered very important circumstantial evidence in identifying the murdered person.

This was followed up by a 'photographic superimposition' achieved under the supervision of Dr V.K. Kashyap, Deputy Director of Central Forensic Sciences Laboratory. This method was first applied in the country in the Pancham Shukla murder case of 1960. This was the second time it was applied, thirty-four years later. The test report said, 'The superimposition test suggests that the skull and the mandible belonged to a person whose photographs were forwarded to me for test.'

During the court hearings, it was hard to counter the

compelling arguments of the police's chargesheet. In 2000, the sessions court ordered death by hanging for Aloknath, Mamata, Shibshankar and Mrinal. The Calcutta High Court verdict was exactly the same. When the case moved to the Supreme Court of India, Alok's punishment was reduced to life imprisonment, and the others, who had by then served sentences for many years, were released. Aloknath recently died in Behrampore Jail.

How does one explain Aloknath's cool disposition? Is it possible to anatomise a cruel killer's mind? To kill a brother only for ill gotten gains, getting rid of the body and sleeping peacefully where the murder was committed!

Arthamanartham! They say money is the root of all evil.

CRUEL INTENTIONS

The Haroun Rasheed murder case, 1994

Park Street police station. Case number 539. Date: 15 August 1994. Indian Penal Code Sections 364, 302, 201, 34: kidnapping or abduction in order to murder, murder, causing disappearance of evidence of offence, acts done by several persons in furtherance of common intention.

'Roll number one?'

'Present, Miss!'

'Roll number two?'

'Yes, Miss!'

'Three?'

'Present, please!'

'Roll number four?'

Silence. Shahnaz, class one teacher at Progressive Day School in central Kolkata's Ripon Street looked up from the attendance register.

'Where's Haroun? Isn't he here?'

'No, Miss. He is absent.'

'Okay, roll number five?'

The roll call continued.

Scenes from busy Indian railway stations are similar in their quotidian details. The same multitude of people, the tireless movement of coolies with boxes, trunks and baggage on the head from one platform to another, announcements in Hindi and English of the arrival and departure of trains every minute, railway engines backing in and out, their laboured chugs…

Each train entered the station, stopped at the platform and disgorged a crowd of people, other trains left with compartments brimming with passengers, the autorickshaw and taxi stands outside the station were filled with groups of chattering drivers. They knew there would not be a dearth of passengers at any hour of the day, whether with the first cawing of crows in the morning hours or at midnight. Silence was forbidden here, cacophony ruled.

Bareilly junction, approximately 250 km from Delhi; one of the five busiest railway stations of Uttar Pradesh. Long distance trains leave for different parts of the country from here as well as scores of local and goods trains and all of it contributes to making Bareilly such a busy railway station.

The Bareilly Government Railway Police (GRP) police station too remained busy round-the-clock as a result. There were ten missing persons complaints to handle on an average every day. Children in particular often got separated from large groups and unless exceptionally unlucky, they were reunited after a bit of search. A big station meant that it was a happy hunting ground for pickpockets. Bareilly was no exception. Dozens of pickpocket complaints poured in every day. As the daylight faded and night took over, the corners and enclosures filled with drunkards and gamblers. The length and breadth of platforms needed surveillance in three shifts—morning, evening, night. There wasn't any scope for a laid-back approach at any part of the day.

It was the juncture between dusk and evening, when two constables inspecting the platform suddenly stumbled upon a rather large steel trunk.

Why was it there? Did a coolie bring it? Did he forget to put it on board the train and the owners lost track of it? Did someone rush to buy something and would come back to claim it soon? But without anyone guarding it, surely they didn't expect to find the trunk when they returned? Better to carry it to the GRP police station, else someone would soon come wailing and whimpering to complain that it had been stolen.

So they carried the steel trunk to the GRP police station. The officer-in-charge thoroughly checked the exterior to see if the owner's name was written on it. Since there was nothing he asked for the lock to be broken. As soon as the lid was opened, the GRP police station staff yelped in terror.

Mohammed Hadis lived with his family on 22/2A Bright Street under Park Street police station limits. He hailed from Bihar's Gaya district and came down to Kolkata in the mid-Eighties, looking for a job. After a lot of legwork, he got himself a job in Ajanta Leathers Fashion Limited, a leather goods factory on Shirazul Islam Lane near Eliot Road. He was a sincere worker—never lethargic or slipshod—qualities that made him a trusted employee within a short time.

They were a small and happy family of nine-year-old Haroun, and a baby girl, his wife and Hadis. Their daughter was so small she didn't even have a proper name—she had several, people had given her so many loving names!

Hadis was so keen on sending his children to Kolkata schools, that he arranged for his wife and children to move from Gaya. The family moved to Kolkata in 1994, when Haroun was nine years old, and he was admitted to class one at Progressive Day School.

School hours were between 7 a.m. and 12 noon, so Hadis would drop his son and go to work, and Haroun would return alone either by tram or by foot. A few hours of sleep, and then he played football every afternoon in the neighbourhood.

August 13 turned out to be different. Haroun didn't return home. The boy who was always home by 12.30 p.m. wasn't back even at three in the afternoon. Where was Haroun? What had happened to him?

Hadis was informed. He rushed home.

First the parents went to the school. The school guard informed them that all the children had long left for the day, and he hadn't noticed whether Haroun was among them. Could he have gone to a friend's place? They searched there too. He had not. Worried neighbours came rushing, office colleagues dropped by. Hadis immediately informed his four closest friends—Mohammed Shamsuddin, Quddus Alam, Mohammed Iqhlaq and long-time neighbour Alamgir—about the crisis.

They had a long association with Hadis. All four men were between thirty and forty years old. Other than Iqhlaq, the others hailed from Gaya, and had come down to Kolkata in search of work. Shamsuddin ran a small garments business and was a friend of many years. Around a year before this event took place, Hadis and Shamsuddin had jointly rented a small two-roomed flat on 36 Aga Mehdi Lane. This was meant for their relatives who often came down to Kolkata on holidays or on work.

Mohammed Iqhlaq hailed from Bihar's Chhapra. He was Hadis's colleague at Ajanta Leathers Fashion Limited, where he had joined on Hadis's recommendation. Iqhlaq was naturally grateful to Hadis for this, and was always the first to rush to his aid whenever there was any need. However, he had been compelled to quit the leather factory job recently, due to prolonged illness. At the time he did some temporary work. He was single and lived with his father in a two-roomed rented apartment on 4, Dedar Bux Lane.

Alamgir ran a motor car parts repairing shop near Eliot Road. He lived with his family on Bright Street, they were close friends and neighbours who often visited each other's place.

The person most worried by the day's development was Quddus Alam, who was Haroun's favourite uncle. Haroun loved Quddus Chacha to bits, and it was he who had introduced the boy to football. Quddus lived at the Aga Mehdi Road flat jointly rented by Hadis and Shamsuddin. Hadis had also got Quddus a temporary, part-time job at Ajanta Leathers Fashion Limited.

When a night-long search in all possible places failed to yield any result, Hadis lodged a missing diary on August 14 at Park Street police station with the general diary entry (GDE) number 1515.

Only, Hadis suppressed a crucial information from the police—a call that had come to him the day before around 3.15 p.m. at his factory.

'Call for you, Hadis-bhai!'

'For me? Who is it?'

'No idea. He didn't give his name.'

Hadis put the receiver against his ears. From the other end came a crackling, hoarse voice that paused several times while uttering a few sentences.

'Your son is with us. Come near the Park Circus bridge number four around ten o'clock tonight. Bring twenty-five thousand rupees in a black bag. Our man will be there in a red cap with a watch on his right hand. Hand over the bag to him. Of course you can inform the police, but then you won't find your son alive. If you hand over the money, your son will be back by tomorrow evening. Another thing: come alone, we don't like smart people.'

A cold shiver ran through Hadis after the line got disconnected. Twenty-five thousand rupees? He earned an average salary, and somehow managed with what he got. It was 3.15 p.m. at the time, how would he get so much cash by 10 p.m.? Hadis was so nervous, he even forgot to ask the caller to allow him to hear Haroun's voice. His endearing 'Abba!' would have calmed him a bit.

Shamsuddin pitched in with two thousand rupees, Quddus and Iqhlaq contributed a thousand rupees each, Alamgir pooled in four thousand rupees from his sources. Hadis's employer, the owner of the factory, who had a soft corner for Hadis stood by him at this difficult time and offered five thousand rupees. The remaining amount was loaned from neighbours and taken from Hadis's own savings.

Park Circus bridge number four was close to Bright Street, so Hadis put twenty-five thousand rupees into a black bag and headed for the destination at 9.30 p.m.

An impatient, jittery Hadis looked every minute, every second at his watch. He patiently waited till 11 p.m., but there was no sign of the man in a red cap with a watch on the right wrist. Hadis didn't want to take chances and waited some more, but when nobody appeared in sight till 11.30 p.m., a dejected Hadis staggered home, heart filled with dread and hopelessness.

He couldn't make sense of anything. Where was the boy?

Who would have kidnapped him and why? The situation at home was frightening. His wife had stopped eating, his tiny daughter was asking after her brother, what was he going to do now?

Relatives and neighbours were playing the same monotonous drone since the time Haroun went missing: 'everything will be fine'. Hadis hated it. What would be fine? How could things be fine if Haroun wasn't found? Only a person who has been separated from their child would know. Where was the boy? How was he doing?

Should he inform the police now? Should he inform them about the ransom call? Wouldn't it be judicious to just file a missing diary and wait for the kidnapper's next call? Perhaps the kidnappers deliberately didn't appear and had kept an eye on him from a distance? Better to wait for a day. What if the kidnappers killed Haroun on learning that the police had been informed? Hadis had to make an effort to divert his mind from such dreadful thoughts.

Thus the information about the ransom call was suppressed before the police while filing the missing diary on the morning of August 14.

And yet, when no call came throughout the entire day despite a long, depressing wait, Hadis returned to Park Street police station that evening along with Shamsuddin, Quddus, Iqhlaq, Alamgir and a few others. He blurted out everything before the officers and lodged a fresh complaint. Sub-inspector Ashique Ahmed (currently officer-in-charge of Topsia police station) was assigned to the probe.

As Hadis stepped out of the police station that evening, he could never have imagined that he would be back again the following day due to the arrival of some dreadful news.

Everything that a school-going child was likely to have was in place—exercise copies inside a school bag, tiffin box, water bottle. The school boy was there too, his uniformed, lifeless body inside the steel trunk.

OC Bareilly GRP police station regarded the body for a few moments, and understood the child had been strangulated. There were clear finger marks on the throat. Easy to find the child's identity too—the exercise copies had his name written on them.

'Sir, the child's name is Haroun Rasheed, student of Progressive Day School from Kolkata.'

'Find out the phone number of this school, quick, and book a call...'

It was 9.30 p.m. on August 15.

~

When the phone call from Bareilly came to Haroun's school at 10.45 p.m., there was only one person in the school to receive it—the guard. He took the call half asleep and was shaken up by what he was told. He immediately informed the principal, who in turn got in touch with Hadis, asking him to rush to Park Street police station.

Park Street OC, Byomkesh Banerjee, spoke with Bareilly GRP OC on the phone. A police team would leave for Bareilly along with Hadis as quickly as possible. Hadis's employer rushed to the police station that night, offering to pay for Hadis's air fare. If they took the early morning flight to Delhi and a car from there, they could reach Bareilly by evening.

They took the morning flight on August 16. Shamsuddin and Alamgir accompanied the distraught father. Hadis's wife had taken to the bed as the news had made her hysteric.

She was talking incoherently and so Quddus and Iqhlaq needed to stay back to manage Hadis's home.

It was late afternoon when the team from Kolkata reached Bareilly.

A glimpse of the body, his little boy's face, and Hadis's world fell apart, his head reeled, he fell unconscious.

The post mortem was conducted in Bareilly and it was found that the boy had indeed been strangulated; no other wounds were found on any other part of the body.

A little boy full of life was kidnapped, and his body found locked inside a trunk a few thousands of kilometres away, in Bareilly station. Such a thing had never happened in the history of the Kolkata Police. Who could have committed such a barbaric act?

Police officers had spoken with Hadis for about an hour on August 15. He had a flight to catch the next morning, and he had plunged into a deathly silence. Yet, some questions had to be asked, no matter how cruel the circumstances.

'Do you have any enemy?'

'No, Sir. I am a simple, family man. I have no enemies.'

'Do you suspect anyone?'

'No, Sir. Why did they kill Haroun, Sir? He had done no one any harm. I can't think of anything. I don't suspect anybody. Why should I? Is it really Haroun's body? Sure there hasn't been any mistake?'

It was obvious that he couldn't think clearly and it was unreasonable to ask him questions and expect clear answers. Investigating officer Ashique dropped Hadis home, and began to think of the various possibilities on his way back.

First, one or many persons involved in the kidnap had asked for ransom to be handed over near Park Circus bridge number four. Why did they not come to take it? Why did they kill the boy without picking up the ransom? This was most surprising.

Two, kidnap and murder for only twenty-five thousand rupees? A professional gang usually had prior information before they ventured into the job. The gang would have known Hadis earned a salary of rupees three thousand only and it would be difficult for him to arrange twenty-five thousand rupees. Did the kidnappers not do their basic homework?

Three, what was the motive? Money was clearly not the issue. Hadis had said he had no enemies. What then? There were more questions he needed to be asked on his return from Bareilly. Was it related to family matters rooted in Gaya? Or, elsewhere? Something related to his workplace?

Four, how did the body reach Bareilly station? Why Bareilly? There were many places in the city and its outskirts to dispose off the body. Haroun had left school on August 13 in the afternoon, and the body was found at Bareilly station on August 15 in the late evening. Did the kidnappers board the Bareilly-bound train from Kolkata? Did they kill him in the train?

Five, a boy was kidnapped from busy Ripon Street during the day, yet nobody noticed it? Wasn't that unusual? Was someone known to the family involved in the crime? He needed to visit the school first thing tomorrow, Ashique decided. Haroun's classmates needed to be asked if they saw something worth mentioning. The guard and other staff in the school required to be interrogated too.

Six, old crime records must be checked even if it required staying up all night. Kidnapping cases of the last five years—how many had been solved, where were the accused now (whether in jail or outside on bail), and photographs of kidnappers had to be taken out from the Crime Records Section (CRS).

Seven, was it a new gang? Kidnapping is not the job of newbies. It requires the expertise of professional gangs. Picking up a child and killing him for a mere twenty-five thousand rupees—the calculation didn't work out. Maybe a new gang was just entering the scene and while twenty-five thousand wasn't a big amount, neither was it a small amount, especially if it involved desperate new entrants.

Eight, it all came back to the same argument—whoever did this monstrous job, hadn't got any money worth the effort. Why then would they kill the child before they got cash? There were instances of killing the kidnapped person *after* collecting the ransom money to get rid of every possibility of identification. But it didn't apply here.

Nine, other than his parents, Haroun had been close to Quddus. He had played with the child almost every day. Ashique needed to talk to Quddus urgently the next day to find out who were Haroun's friends, what he loved to eat, other likes and dislikes—all important for the investigation.

Shamsuddin, Alamgir and Iqhlaq would be interrogated too. These men were close to the family and could give important information. Hadis's wife, once she got a grip on herself, had to be asked certain questions as well. Investigations involved such embarrassing work like placing questions before the mother of a child who had been killed but then, how else could one unearth the truth? It is difficult to understand something from the placid surface, perhaps the motive behind the murder was not ransom money, but something else?

16 August 1994, Monday, 7.45 a.m. Slowly, the city was waking up to the first day of the week.

It was the first period at Progressive Day School. Ashique reached the school with a couple of officers and Quddus.

Once inside the school premises, Ashique had a preliminary discussion with the school's principal. The news wasn't yet out in the newspapers, but it would certainly leak out during the day and the next day's papers would carry the shocking news of the abduction and murder of a nine-year-old child. The police officers asked the school authorities not to disclose matters to the children before that—there was no need to scare them.

A list of all teachers and non-teaching staff was required. Also, it was important to talk to the children of class one; when would it be convenient for the school to allow the officers a conversation?

The moment Ashique entered the classroom, he realized what a silly thing he had done—he was in uniform! The children of class one, tiny little humans sitting on benches with their school books and exercise copies, their innocent faces full of wonder, were now unsettled to see policemen entering their classroom.

'The police uncle will ask you something. Don't worry! There's no need to be afraid.'

It was clear that class teacher Shahnaz's assurance didn't have any impact on the children and they continued to be filled with dread. But Ashique decided to go ahead anyway. There was no way he could turn around and run, so he tried to frame his questions tactfully.

'Your friend Haroun is absent even today. Perhaps he is hiding somewhere, that naughty little Haroun! But his parents are so worried, you know! When he left school last Friday, were any of you with him?'

Pin drop silence.

'Can any of you recall which way Haroun went after school? Did any of you accompany him that day?'

Not a word.

Ashique left the classroom. This wouldn't work with children. Tomorrow or day after, some police officers in civil clothes would be sent to talk to the children during lunchtime. First they needed to break the ice. Right now, he wanted to check with the school authorities if anyone from the same school lived close to Haroun's place. If there were such children, they could give definitive clues.

He was back in the principal's room, where some senior teachers were discussing security issues. It was time to introduce rules to prevent students from leaving the school unless guardians came to pick them up. Shahnaz's voice interrupted the discussion.

'Sir, there's something...'

The principal looked at her. A little boy stood by her, fear writ large on his tiny face.

'Sir, Shabir is Haroun's classmate. He wants to say something to Mr Ashique. He was afraid to speak a little while ago...'

Ashique stood up. Did the child see something? What did he want to say? Would this boy offer something important?

'Uncle, last Friday, Haroun and I left school together. We do that everyday.'

'What happened on Friday?'

'When I reached home and said "bye" to Haroun, someone called him.'

'Where is your home?'

'Close by.'

'Then?'

'Then Haroun happily left with that man.'

'Happily?'

'Yes, happily!'

'Can you recognize the man if you see him again?'

'Yes, Sir!'

'Not Sir, call me Uncle.'

As Ashique lightly patted the child's cheeks, feeling grateful, his mind had started working on the next step in the investigation. If the boy had seen the man, it was necessary to draw a sketch with his description. The child had finally offered a ray of hope. Surely he deserved a chocolate.

Shahnaz came out of the principal's room, holding the boy's hand. Ashique, the principal and other teachers followed them. Ashique called out, 'Quddus, go bring a chocolate for this boy! Quick!'

Quddus was standing near the police vehicle parked outside the school gate. He turned around when Ashique called out to him from about twenty feet away. Suddenly, Shabir pressed Shahnaz's hand.

'What's the matter, child?'

'Miss, that uncle! Haroun happily went with that uncle on Friday!'

Ashique was thunderstruck. So was Quddus. For a

fraction of a second, they had eye contact. Then Quddus began to run. 'Catch him!' Ashique yelled at the officer standing by the police vehicle.

The driver too understood instantly and jumped out of the car. Quddus had nowhere to run. In any case, how far could he have gone?

~

Quddus? Haroun's Quddus Chacha? Why?

'I didn't do it alone, Sir. Iqhlaq was there too.'

Quddus said these words softly, sitting on the floor of the Park Street OC's chamber, chin down, head resting on his folded legs. That very moment, a car started off for Iqhlaq's Dedar Bux Lane address.

'Why did you murder a child?'

Quddus's narrative revealed the details of a shocking drama, and the motive behind the murder stunned the officers. How could there be such a trivial reason behind a murder?

'Iqhlaq and I were recommended by Hadis-bhai for jobs in his factory. Basically, Hadis-bhai looked up to Shamsuddin-bhai and would do anything he asked of him. Shamsuddin-bhai was a distant relative of Iqhlaq and me, and naturally, our well-wisher, so he requested Hadis-bhai to recommend our names in his factory, and Hadis-bhai couldn't turn him down.'

'So you repaid debt by murdering that person's child?'

Quddus hid his face in his hands.

'A devil had got into my head! I didn't want to get involved in this. I fell for Iqhlaq's plan....'

'Aha! You say that now because you fell into the net before him. Had he come into our clutches first, he would have said the same thing about you—that you had hatched the plan. We know such tricks. Come on, tell us why did you kill the child?'

'Earlier I would make do with whatever I could manage from here and there, asking people for money… Once I began to earn a salary, Iqhlaq and I started drinking almost every day. We would often be late to work. One day, the supervisor had an angry outburst, and handed us notices for not fulfilling our duties. We ran to Shamsuddin-bhai, he approached Hadis in turn, asking him to take up the matter. Hadis requested the factory owner to give us another chance. He loved Hadis blindly, so he gave us another chance just to honour his request, and our job was saved.'

'Then?'

'We worked sincerely for a while, but then were back to our old ways. Iqhlaq was a heavy drinker and soon fell ill. He went back to his Chhapra home, and stayed there for six months. When he returned a month ago and went back to the factory asking to be re-inducted, the owner flatly refused. Iqhlaq would drink even at work, Hadis-bhai had in fact, requested him many times to not do that, but he paid no heed to his advice.

'Iqhlaq approached Shamsuddin-bhai all over again. This time, Hadis-bhai put his foot down. He was very clear, "I warned you repeatedly, but you didn't change yourself. The owner engaged you just to honour my request and gave you one last chance, but you made light of it. How will I approach him again? Better that you find yourself another job." There was a lot of argument over this.'

'That may be Iqhlaq's logic, but you had your job!'

'What job, Sir! It was temporary, part-time work. The

owner refused to make it a permanent job. The supervisor had reported to him that I went late to work, and that I didn't work sincerely. When Iqhlaq wasn't re-inducted, I got all the more worried and I approached Hadis-bhai, "If you say it once, my job will be permanent. The salary will increase, how can one manage with such a measly sum? It's impossible to make ends meet."

'Hadis-bhai snapped at me, "Keep working sincerely for at least a year. Didn't you see what happened to Iqhlaq? Everybody knows about the two of you. There's no chance of making your job permanent. If you push a bit more, you'll lose out on what you have now."

'I went mad with anger. That very day I quit the job and told Hadis-bhai, "I don't need your kindness, I don't need a job you've given me. My foot!" Hadis lost his cool too. He said, "It was my mistake to recommend your names."'

'Hmm.'

'There can be such quarrels, I didn't take it to heart, Sir. We even made up. I would drop in at Hadis-bhai's place and take Haroun to the football ground. But Iqhlaq couldn't forget the anger and hurt caused to him due to the loss of his job. One day, he called me to his Dedar Bux Lane rooms, we drank till late into the night and Iqhlaq poured poison into my heart.'

'And you allowed him to do it?'

'I was out of my mind, Sir. I was jobless. Iqhlaq thought that Hadis-bhai could have easily recommended our names to his bosses if he wanted to, and that we were both jobless because of him. We must seek revenge by turning his life topsy-turvy, he said. I was so overcome with ghastly thoughts, I agreed.

'We planned it out together—that we'd kidnap Haroun and demand twenty-five thousand rupees, return to our respective villages and start a business. Haroun had to be killed because he knew us.'

'But you never went to get the ransom you asked for. Why?'

'How could we? The day we picked up Haroun, we were accompanying Hadis-bhai in search of the boy since evening. We searched everywhere so people wouldn't suspect us. Hadis-bhai left with the ransom money around 9.30 p.m. telling us, "Please look after Bhabi-jaan and the girl." We couldn't leave Bright Street as their house was full of people and all of them were in tears. Our plan didn't work out.'

'When did you kill Haroun?'

~

13 August 1994. School was over and Haroun and Shabir were walking home like they did every day.

Quddus was on the prowl near a shop close to Shabir's home on Abdul Latif Street. Iqhlaq watched from afar. When Quddus saw Haroun, he called out to him from a distance and the child, excited to see his favourite uncle on the way home, demanded an ice-cream treat.

Quddus said, 'All right, come, let's go to my place and I'll treat you to one and then I'll drop you home.' Iqhlaq joined them as they started off. Though Haroun was not very familiar or comfortable with him, he knew of him as his father's and Quddus-chacha's friend.

The two of them took Haroun to the rented flat of 36 Aga Mehdi Lane, the plan being to first murder the boy there. However, on the way, they met a neighbour who squeezed the boy's cheeks affectionately. This necessitated a change of plan, as both decided it wouldn't be wise to keep a witness to Haroun's entry into the house.

So they took him to the Dedar Bux Lane flat, explaining to Haroun that Iqhlaq-chacha had ice-cream at his place.

On the way, they met yet another familiar face from the neighbourhood, Sheikh Shahabuddin, who owned a vegetable shop on Dedar Bux Lane and knew both Hadis and Haroun. Shahabuddin asked the child, 'Would you like to have a toffee?' Haroun refused, 'No! I'm going for ice-cream. I will go home after that.'

Ice-cream? There was no ice-cream for little Haroun. The moment he entered the flat, Haroun heard Quddus-chacha telling Iqhlaq, 'No point of wasting any more time, let's finish him off.'

Quddus and Iqhlaq nabbed the child's throat and twisted it, squeezing the life out of him. How long would it have taken for Haroun to die? A few minutes perhaps. What good was his little strength to fight the physical power and sinister intent of two devils?

They were well prepared. Quddus had bought a huge steel trunk a few days ago and kept it in his Aga Mehdi Lane home. However, due to the change of plan, he had to take a rickshaw to bring the trunk to Iqhlaq's place. They put Haroun's body into the trunk and locked it.

As planned, the trunk was taken out, and on the way they made a ransom call from a public telephone booth on Paymental Garden Lane, then hired a taxi to Howrah station.

The trunk was placed in a ladies' compartment of Kathgodam Express, which departed from Howrah station at 4.17 p.m. It reached Bareilly forty-eight hours later. Once the passengers left, a cleaner noticed the trunk and thought someone had perhaps left it behind by mistake, so he placed it on the platform.

The trunk was soon spotted by the railway police personnel on surveillance duty.

The investigation after Quddus's arrest was handled by Sub-Inspector Bikash Chattopadhyay from the homicide section under Kolkata Police's detective department. Chattopadhyay retired a few years ago as Assistant Commissioner.

On learning about Quddus's arrest, Iqhlaq fled the state. He turned out to be sharper at being on the run than he had ever been at performing his job. It wasn't easy to catch him. Sleuths searched for him and laid traps for him for days all over Bihar. Finally, in October-end, he came down to Kolkata for a couple of days, making sure he had taken all the precautions to remain hidden from the police's sharp eyes but reliable police sources informed the officers about this secret arrival. Iqhlaq was sent straight to prison.

Bikash Chattopadhyay didn't like to keep any 'chance factor' in his investigation and was respected by his juniors and seniors alike for the extra effort he put in to make every aspect of the probe nothing less than perfect.

This was Bikash's style of cautious handling where no loopholes were tolerated.

He had prepared the witnesses' statements and evidence with perfect precision, so that the accused couldn't ever dream of getting away.

Quddus had bought the trunk for Rs 220 from a shop

in Mullickbazar. He had himself directed the police to this shop, so a copy of the cash memo was retrieved by the Lalbazar sleuths. The shopkeeper identified him in court as the man who had bought the trunk from his shop.

During interrogation, Quddus also led the police to the public telephone booth from where he and Iqhlaq had made the ransom call. Wasim Mubarki, the shop owner, identified both. This was substantiated by the telephone call list in possession of the shop owner which clearly indicated that a call had been made to Hadis's factory on August 13 at 3.15 p.m.

Taxi drivers who were regulars around Ripon Street helped police locate the driver and the taxi in which Quddus and Iqhlaq had taken the trunk to Howrah station. The driver (with the taxi number plate WB-04/2052) Mohammed Akbar, agreed to be a witness in the case. He told the court he had driven the two men from the area to the station carrying a rather bulky steel trunk.

All their deeds were corroborated by many others who had spotted them that afternoon. The rickshaw puller, Mohammed Shamsad, who took Quddus from Aga Mehdi Lane to Deodar Bux Lane carrying the empty trunk; Quddus's neighbour who had seen Haroun with Quddus and Iqhlaq; and the vegetable shop owner from Deodar Bux Lane who had offered a lolly to Haroun.

Haroun's friend Shabir Rahman was perhaps the most important witness in this case. He recalled how the two friends had come out of the school gate together, and Haroun had 'happily' left with the uncle. Shabir did not dither for a second. In court he pointed to Quddus and said, 'That uncle!'

The verdict came in 2003. Quddus and Iqhlaq were

proven guilty and given life imprisonment. The higher court even turned down the subsequent appeal.

As P.D. James wrote in *The Murder Room*, 'All the motives for murder are covered by the four Ls: Love, Lust, Lucre and Loathing'.

So true! Haroun was victim to the last L. What abominable loathing!

A TOUGH NUT TO CRACK

The Ramzan Ali murder case, 1994

Park Street police station. Case number 825. Date: 20 December 1994. Indian Penal Code Sections 302, 34, 394, 397: murder, acts done by several persons in furtherance of common intention, voluntarily causing hurt in committing robbery, robbery or dacoity with attempt to cause death or grievous hurt.

Lalbazar Control Room, 20 December 1994, 1.45 a.m.

The sound of the telephone ringing shattered the silence. The night-shift officer picked up the receiver.

'Why is there such delay? This is OC Park Street. Send in the forces, quick!'

'They have left a while ago. Will reach any time now.'

'Note down the location. Send more forces. As quickly as possible. It's getting difficult to handle the situation now.'

'Roger.'

The Control Room sprang into hyperactivity. The shift in-charge, an experienced hand, was quick to figure out that this was going to be a gruelling night. He lifted the walkie-talkie, its loud crackles filled the air. 'Control Room calling. Heavy Radio Flying Squad Ten, location please?'

'Replying, approaching Indian Museum.'

'Report to the OC on reaching. Deputy Commissioner South is on the way.'

It was a bitterly cold night. The months of Poush and

Maagh in the Bengali calendar corresponding with parts of December and January of the Gregorian were not superficial and snazzy like the quick-fix twenty-twenty cricket matches played these days. Those biting cold nights were tough players that refused to let go of the crease. They made one snuggle down under the warmth of comforters and would not give up easily. Outside, it was difficult to manage without full-sleeved woollens or shawls.

When the additional force reached the spot, the initial lot of police force was already floundering about. The place had begun to fill up. Curious onlookers were gathering outside the gate, making every attempt to enter the premises, but were being met with stern resistance from the police. A chaos was waiting to break out.

News of the murder had just filtered out, and a forensic team was on the way, many senior IPS officers had reached already, and political bigwigs had started pouring in. The place was choc-a-bloc with beacon-light flashing cars.

Thankfully there were no twenty-four-hour television news channels at the time. Else, things would have been much more difficult for the police to handle with the shoving and jostling of cameras and booms competing with each other in an incredible rat race to telecast 'breaking news' and 'exclusive's every minute and second! But even in those Doorsharshan-dominated days, a group of journalists—mostly from various newspapers—were already there, even if it was well past midnight.

A little past three in the morning a woman in her mid-thirties, her face white as a sheet, was assisted towards the main gate of the building. The suddenness of the event had so baffled her, she seemed drained of all energy, reduced to a staggering spectre unable to walk on her own. Her high cheekbones, eyes sunken into hollows, thin frame slouched, trembling lips—all of it indicated the turmoil inside.

The police had a lot of work ahead—preparing a detailed sketch map of the incident spot, list names of those to be interrogated immediately, make a list of items procured from where the body was found, send the body for post mortem at the crack of dawn (so a preliminary report indicating the method of killing could arrive by evening) and so on. And of course, they needed to register a First Information Report (FIR) based on the statement of the woman who had just witnessed her husband's murder.

The journalists, too, were frightfully busy. They needed to get back to their respective offices and quickly file reports on the incident so that it could be carried in at least the late city edition (the early edition had by then been printed already). This was, after all, front page news!

~

It was nearly 3.45 a.m. when the woman was made to sit in the chamber of the Park Street officer-in-charge. The night would be over soon, milky rays of dawn would cleanse the remaining darkness around. Women police personnel were trying to console as much as it was possible, a woman who had just witnessed her husband being strangulated. The Deputy Commissioner of detective department was himself present at the police station. The air was taut with suspense. After a lot of goading, she was barely able to utter a few words '*Mein to bilkul akeli ho gayi... life barbaad ho gaya...*' (I am now all alone...my life has turned topsy-turvy) Saying this, she burst into another bout of wailing.

'Calm down, Madam! Please tell us, what exactly happened?'

Her ashen face delineated the terror she had witnessed less than a few hours ago. Finally she began to utter a few more words. This was Talat Sultana, wife of Ramzan Ali, Forward Bloc lawmaker from Goalpokhor in Uttar Dinajpur district.

'We stay at the MLA Hostel on Kyd Street whenever we come down to Kolkata. This time was no exception. I have been with Ramzan saheb since December 13; we've come here for his medical treatment. We were in Room 3/10 on the third floor.

'Yesterday, at around 12.30 p.m., Subba-didi—Renulina Subba, former lawmaker of the All India Gorkha League—came to us with a request. All the rooms had been booked, so she wanted to know if we would let her stay with us. I have known her for many years, Ramzan saheb knew her for even longer, so he said, "Of course! Do stay with us."

'So she kept her luggage in our room and left. She was back at 6 p.m. She went out again, around 9.15 p.m. to buy some medicines, and we all had dinner together when she was back after a while. Subba-didi slept at 10 p.m. In fifteen minutes to half an hour, Ramzan saheb and I too fell asleep. It was around 11.30 p.m. when we were both woken up by sounds of knocking on the door. Subba-didi was in deep sleep, so the sounds did not wake her. Ramzan saheb asked me to open the door, suggesting that it could be Matin and perhaps it was related to work.

'Matin is a whole-timer of the Forward Bloc party. He and Alam had put up in Room 1/8. I opened the door and peered out. No, there was nobody there. Hadn't there been any noise? Ramzan saheb asked me to keep the door unlocked, as he was sure it was Matin who had knocked.

There were some pending discussions on party matters, he may have knocked but left thinking we were asleep.

'I did not bolt the door and went to the balcony adjoining the room, thinking it would be best to do the dishes since my sleep had been disturbed anyway. Just as I was clearing the dishes, someone came and held my mouth with an iron grip. There were two men, pistol in hand. They held the gun at my throat, forced a blanket on my face and tied my hands and legs with cloth. They dragged me on the floor and took me inside. By then, two more men had entered the room. I was nearly dead with fear. Subba-didi and Ramzan saheb had both been woken up by all the noise. Then they tied her up in the same way and threatened us that they would bump us off if we made any noise.

'They picked up a sari from the clothes stand and began to wind it around Ramzan saheb's throat. I ran to stop them, but one of them kicked me hard on the abdomen and started abusing me, "You bitch!" By then, Ramzan saheb was struggling hard but the assailants showed no pity. "There's a meeting on the 10th, isn't there? See what fun it can be?"

One of them asked me, "Where's the money?" Then, without waiting for my reply, picked up the purse lying on top of a suitcase and took out everything from it. All this happened within half an hour, with constant threats of killing me if I made any noise.

'After they had left, Subba-didi and I crawled and dragged ourselves to the intercom. Ramzan saheb wasn't making any noise at all—he was lying motionless—and I went stiff with fear.

'Subba-didi and I both worked hard to untie our hands.

Finally, after a lot of effort, we could open the knots that held my hands together. I called Matin's room and he and Alam came running. They opened all our fastenings. Ramzan saheb did not make any movement even when Matin opened the knots wound around his throat. Matin then checked his pulse, put his hand near the nostrils to check if he was breathing, but by then, he was foaming from the mouth. Matin told us, "Ramzan bhai is no more."

'Everything happened right in front of my eyes, Sir... I'll be able to identify them... please hound them out and punish them...' Talat said.

Then she broke into sobs again.

After such a long, unbroken narration Talat became breathless and dizzy with exhaustion. The DC-DD extended a glass of water towards her. 'Drink some water, Madam. You need to rest. We'll put in our best efforts to catch the murderers, I give you my word.' She looked blankly into space, as if the words had not even reached her.

Park Street is one of the most popular destinations for Kolkata visitors. If you move south towards Park Street from Jawaharlal Nehru Road, you will find Kyd Street on the left. A few metres from the main road, and the MLA Hostel will be on your right. A glow sign with the words, 'Bidhan Sabha Sadashya, Abas Bibhag' (Members of Legislative Assembly, Housing Department) attached to the high iron grilled main gate won't go unnoticed. The compound is guarded round the clock by armed sentries, including its main gate.

How could a lawmaker be brutally murdered in the middle of the night in a place that ought to have had foolproof security? There was a lot of brouhaha over this lapse, quite naturally. The media would not let go of such an opportunity to lambast the police. There were allegations and outrage over the fact that despite the spectacle of police personnel apparently guarding the place, the real security had been nothing but an eyewash. It led to furore and turmoil in the state's politics.

The Forward Bloc party, whose Member of Legislative Assembly Ramzan Ali was, threatened to call a state-wide bandh if the murderers were not caught within forty-eight hours. This had to be dealt with a lot of care and priority. Two special teams were formed at Lalbazar, the Kolkata Police headquarters, each of these headed by top officers. Within two days, not unexpectedly, the detective department was asked to investigate the case.

Mohammed Akram, Inspector in the homicide section was appointed investigating officer for the case. A smart detective, patient investigator, and a shrewd officer, Akram had a nose for clues. Others in his team envied this aspect of Akram's working style—he always got lucky in finding clues from the least expected places. That's exactly how he would eventually get to the bottom of this case too. After an exciting stint in the homicide section, he retired as Deputy Commissioner in the Armed Police's Eighth Battalion. No matter how heroic their achievements are, police investigators always remain low-key and anonymous—that's their style of functioning.

The investigation started. The post mortem report quite predictably mentioned the cause of death as manual strangulation.

Room Number 3/10 in the MLA Hostel was quite ordinary. The rooms here do not compare with plush suites in hotels. The modest rooms have two single beds, an adjoining kitchen and a bathroom. The MLA Hostel offers cheap accommodation for Members of the Legislative Assembly when they come down to Kolkata from various parts of West Bengal during the Assembly sessions. In fact, they can book rooms there all through the year.

The main door leads to a ten-feet-by-eight-feet space separated from the main room with heavy curtains. The curtains make it impossible for those in the room to see this separated space, and vice versa, unless these were moved by someone.

No foot, hand or sole marks could be developed as vital clues from this room despite thorough scrutiny. A number of things strewn around in the room were picked up by investigators, but none of these could offer any clear direction. Talat had said she would be able to identify the killers, so she was asked to describe them and their sketches were drawn and distributed among police stations and police sources. Nothing. No progress in investigation.

A clue was all that was required. How would the investigation move to the next level? Employees of the MLA Hostel, those who had dropped by that day, all the 'visitors', were interrogated repeatedly, all the meaningful details were looked into, but no path ahead was visible in sight.

In difficult cases, police tend to review the progress of the investigation at regular intervals—it may be every two to three days, or morning, noon and night—it depends on various factors such as the importance of the case or its progress. This one belonged to the second category, one that had led to sleepless nights for the police force.

In one such review meeting three days into the murder, the following conversation took place between the investigating officer and his colleague:

'Sir, I am having serious doubts about Talat Sultana's statement.'

'Since day one as far as I am concerned...'

'Right, Sir! Why should Ramzan ask to keep the door unbolted despite learning that Matin wasn't there?'

'More important, Matin is saying he got a call after 1 a.m.'

'And according to Talat's statement, the murder was committed between 11.30 p.m. and midnight. Even the post mortem report confirms that.'

'Correct. What was she doing for so long?'

'She says it took her long to open the fastenings of her arms. She claims she made the calls after she managed to disentangle the knots.'

'Hmm. Had it been a criminal gang, they would have snapped the telephone lines before leaving.'

'Perhaps they missed it in a hurry?'

'You are missing the most important point here. There were police personnel guarding the premises outside. One doesn't need to sign the registration book only if they go in with someone very familiar with the security personnel. How is it possible that four armed men entered without anyone, not even someone from the reception, noticing them?'

'Maybe the sentries and the constables had dozed off? It was a winter night, after all, maybe the trespassers had taken advantage of that...'

'Talat has said that she heard the first knocks around 11.30 p.m. The sentry duty changed about forty-five minutes before that. It is unlikely they would doze off the moment they took charge. This is acceptable at 2 or 2.30 in the morning...'

'She said she'll be able to identify the assailants. She

gave detailed descriptions of their faces. But the lights were off in the room. How did she manage to see them in such detail?'

'Hmm. That's the most alarming part...'

'How about arresting Talat? Surely she must be hiding *something*! And Renuleena? How is it that she too saw nothing?'

'Talat can be arrested... but it is a bit risky for sure. There is no proof against her, and she is the complainant... however, she can be interrogated again... I think I'll tell the DC about it...'

'Yes, Sir, you must! This pressure is getting a bit much. The newspapers are after us, claiming that this is a political murder. Talat has left for Kishangunj... but here we are, facing the heat.'

'Is this how political murders are committed? There were so many opportunities for murdering the man. As a lawmaker he was meeting people in public places, interacting with people, holding meetings, organizing processions and marches...why should four assailants come down in the middle of the night in a place as secure as the MLA Hostel that is manned by police sentries to murder him? Isn't it quite outrageous? Absurd, even?'

'That's what appears suspicious! She is deliberately misleading us. We must inform the DC.'

The DC was informed. Things were presented from all angles, arguments and counter-arguments, the whole perspective was delineated. Arresting Talat would attract a lot of vituperation from all fronts. But there were far too many holes in her alibi to not take this risk. A court's nod was taken for her arrest warrant. A team led by the DC-DD left for Bihar on December 24. She was arrested from her home in Kishangunj's Bahadurpur, and brought to Kolkata on December 26.

An elaborate questionnaire had been prepared so that she could be caught on the wrong foot. Funnily enough, there was no need for it. After ten minutes of questioning, Talat confessed, her voice cold and devoid of compassion or regret, 'Yes, I admit I had lied. Rabi is the murderer. Ramzan saheb's confidential assistant.'

'Why did he do it?'

'I won't tell you. I'll explain everything before the court.'

'Will you agree to a judicial confession?'

'Yes, sure. Please arrange it.'

'We'll make all the arrangements. But why did you not tell us the truth earlier? What is your connection with Rabi?'

'I told you, I'll give my statement only before the court. Rabi used to address me as "Didi", sister. I have nothing to do with this murder.'

As scheduled, Talat Sultana appeared before the court to offer her judicial confession. It all preceded with the customary promise: 'Whatever I say is the truth and nothing but the truth...'

And what did she tell the court? Here goes:

'I have nothing to do with this murder. I am an ordinary housewife, mother of two daughters and a son. There were municipal polls in Uttar Dinajpur district on May 15. The night before, on May 14, there was a political clash in Hogolbari, in which my late husband, Mohammed Ramzan Ali, was injured. Rabi was his personal assistant, who used to accompany him at all times, he was like his shadow. After his injury, Ramzan saheb was taken to Kolkata, admitted to Calcutta Hospital. After his treatment, when he was released from the hospital, we moved to the MLA

Hostel for some time. All this while, I did everything in my powers to nurse him back to good health. But he always ill-treated me, was cold and aloof. During this time, Rabi helped me a lot, and we were drawn to each other. Before we knew it, we found ourselves in an illicit relationship.

'Soon we were back in Kishangunj. One day, Ramzan saheb saw me and Rabi in a compromising situation, and started abusing me right in front of Rabi, and sacked him immediately. Since then, Rabi has been baying for his blood. As for me, I eventually realized the grave mistake I had committed by being untrue to my husband and stopped all communication with this man.

'I repeat. I have no connection whatsoever, with this murder. Rabi has murdered Ramzan saheb.

'On December 20, Subba-didi, Ramzan saheb and I were in the room. Subba-didi helped Ramzan saheb put some eye drops, then, she slept on one of the beds. My husband was on the other bed. I had prepared to sleep on the floor and had spread a rug. The light was switched off, but the door wasn't locked.

'All of a sudden, I saw Rabi in our room. He had opened the door, moved the curtains and entered. "I have come to check on Kaku… how is he doing?" He always addressed Ramzan saheb as Kaku, or uncle. The very sight of Rabi got my husband's blood boiling. He snapped at me and said, "This haramjada has come to stoke the wild fling he is having with you". Rabi could not quell his anger beyond this point, so he yelled at Ramzan saheb, "You have ruined Didi's life!" Saying this, he pounced on my husband. I rushed and tried to stop him, but he pushed me so hard, I fell on the floor and became unconscious.

'After a while, when I regained consciousness, I found myself lying on the bed where Subba-didi was, my mouth tied with Ramzan saheb's shirt and vest. Subba-didi's face was tied with her red shawl. A sari had been used to strangle MLA saheb, my husband… I… I don't know anything beyond what I have told you just now.

'I have a weak heart, but my ailments have been of no concern to my husband. But I have never done anything less than the best for his treatment and care. Even our last visit to Kolkata was for *his* medical treatment.'

Talat's astonishing claims and revelations stunned everyone. No one in court spoke a word for a few moments.

After a patient hearing, the magistrate asked Talat Sultana, with concern and worry, 'So why did you not disclose all this to the police earlier?'

Talat was nonplussed. She was, after all, giving a bona fide statement this time and oozing confidence. 'I was a bit rattled at first,' she admitted. Then, she decided to add another line to make her explanation and reasoning sound. 'Moreover, I did not want Rabi to be punished. I used to love him. Yet, when I thought this over, I was overcome with guilt and remorse. It would have been a grave injustice if I didn't disclose the truth.' Her eyes were brimming with tears.

Phew! What a relief! Finally the murder mystery had been solved. This is how police tend to react when the accused come up with judicial confessions before the court.

But this respite for the investigators did not last long. When a copy of the judicial confession under Code of Criminal Procedure (CrPC) 164 came to the police, they were flabbergasted! What an embarrassment this was going to be!

Not only were there major contradictions in what Talat had told the police in her FIR and the judicial confession, there were gaping holes in the narrative of the judicial confession too.

Why did you keep the door unlocked at 11 p.m.? Why did Rabi come down to the MLA Hostel after so many years to inquire after Kaku's health? There was no mention of Matin's presence. Talat had mentioned that she fell on the floor and turned unconscious. But there were no marks of injury especially not on her head immediately after the incident. The sleuths agreed unanimously that this lady was a tough nut to crack. She was smart and obviously a raconteur of tall tales.

Unable to outsmart her, the police decided to first get Rabi. His interrogation would provide them the chance to separate the wheat from the chaff.

Rabi Sikdar, age: mid thirties. He was arrested from his house in Nadia district and brought to Kolkata.

What happened next was beyond the imagination of seasoned investigators. Rabi had worked as Ramzan's driver for a while, subsequently he had been his personal assistant too. Several months before his death, however, Ramzan had appointed another driver and Rabi had since returned to his native home and concentrated on farming. After he lost his job, he hadn't been in touch with Talat at all. Rabi told the officers that he'd always addressed Talat as Didi, and there was not even a whiff of romance between them.

He very clearly stated that he was in his Nadia home on the day of the murder, and his last visit to Kolkata had been six months earlier. A police team went to Rabi's Nadia home to establish this claim. They found his statement to be true. There was enough alibi to convince them that he was speaking the truth. Therefore, they did not oppose Rabi's bail plea and he was released.

Imagine the discomfiture of the police now. Newspapers had by then splashed stories of Talat's confession, Rabi's arrest, and how a wild rage had prompted Talat's former paramour to murder the lawmaker. Now, with Rabi's release, the Kolkata Police was slammed for sloppy handling of the case. Another round of fresh attack by the media.

What now?

Start from scratch, no matter how futile the attempt turned out to be, no matter how embarrassing a reminder it was of one's failure. There was in fact, no other option. After a lot of deliberation, Lalbazar decided on three things mainly:

One, all those present at the MLA Hostel that night including all guests, employees, also owners and employees of shops within one kilometre radius of the MLA Hostel were to be interrogated again. Maybe they would remember something they had missed during earlier questioning?

Two, all call records in public telephone booths within a two to three kilometre radius surrounding the MLA Hostel needed to be checked thoroughly. The records of twenty days before the day of murder should be tabulated. Who had called the various guests staying at the MLA Hostel? Not just the boarders of room number 3/10, this should apply to every single room.

Three, teams should be sent to Uttar Dinajpur and Kishangunj. The Forward Bloc party workers had already been interrogated, but no one had breathed out a word. More thorough probing was required on this aspect—local sources should be deployed to tap information, to find every detail of Ramzan Ali's family from the grassroots level. Were there property disputes, would anyone benefit politically from his death? Were there undercurrents of strain in Talat and Ramzan's marriage? How turbulent was the marriage?

Armed with this three-pronged strategy, the officers of Lalbazar were raring to go. The truth had to be unearthed this time.

Soon, the result of hard work, patience, diligence, and intelligent strategizing bore fruit.

Akram decided to make a round of the public telephone booths himself—ten to twelve booths on an average per day—and check out the call lists in detail. The first serious clue came from there.

It was a balmy evening towards the end of January. Akram had had a long and tiring day as he had been going around checking phone booths, apart from other sundry jobs relating to the investigation since morning. Tired to the bone, Akram decided he would check three more booths, then call it a day.

3C Chowringhee Lane. A tiny store with a public call office (PCO), owned by Ranjit Das. He welcomed Akram, offered him a seat and some tea. He handed him the call list, and started chatting about this and that.

Akram noticed from the corner of his eyes that Ranjit Das looked around cautiously, brought his face close to Akram's ears and whispered so no one around could hear what he was saying. 'Sir,' Das began, clearing his throat. 'You've been checking up on the calls made from all PCOs in this area. This is about the MLA murder case, isn't it?'

'Hmm...'

'May I say something, Sir?'

Akram looked up expectantly from the sheet he

was examining. He wasn't very enthusiastic about the conversation, but neither was he unresponsive. He kept going back to the list, knowing that was his main job and that he had no time to waste in idle chatter.

Ranjit's voice was now softer than a whisper.

'Sir, Madam often used to drop by at my booth. I know her quite well.'

'Which Madam?'

'The MLA saheb's Mrs.'

Akram now looked up from the list. He sensed he had reached a major turnaround in the investigation.

'Where would she call?'

'Long distance call, Sir. To Delhi.'

'What's the number? When did she last call the number?'

'Please wait for ten minutes, Sir. I'll take out the list. She was here about a month ago. Yes, I remember quite clearly. Another cup of tea, Sir?'

Tea or sweet nectar drops from heaven, Akram had lost all appetite at that point. His condition was delicate, almost vulnerable for his heart was beating fast, veins pulsating with excitement, arteries throbbing with anticipation.

Talat had made many calls to a Delhi number—011-738624—between October 20 and December 15. The duration of the calls varied from four to ten minutes. Akram dialled the number from the booth now. It was the office of Mumbai Trading Company, owned by Kalim Khan. Akram quickly inquired from Khan about his employees—was there anyone from West Bengal or Bihar working for him?

'*Haan. Bangaal se ek hai. Nurul. Nurul Islam. Sola taarikh se chhutti liya tha. Laut ke nahi aya. Koi gadbad hai kya?*' (Yes, there's someone from Bengal. Nurul Islam.

He has been on leave since the sixteenth, and he has not returned. Is there a problem?)

Akram didn't waste a moment. He quickly left for Lalbazar, had a quick word with the DC-DD, and a team from Lalbazar took a train to Delhi that night.

They also concluded that if Nurul was the murderer, he would have stayed in a hotel surrounding the MLA Hostel on Kyd Street during the time of the murder. Accordingly, most hotels and dharamshalas in south and central Kolkata were to be raided that very night. There ought to be someone by the name Nurul Islam or an alias who had checked into a hotel on December 16 or 17 and stayed on till December 20.

If the chosen track is right, it doesn't take long to find the hidden gems. After three hours or so of frenetic searching, Nurul Islam's name was found in the register at Khwaja Habib Hotel a stone's throw from the MLA Hostel. He had checked in on the morning of the 19th, mentioned he would be there till the 22nd morning, but midway through the stay, he cleared all bills and left on 20th night around 10 p.m.

The following day, another important clue came to light in a way that enraged and elated the investigators at the same time. This doesn't happen quite so often in complicated probes. For some days, a team from Lalbazar had been interrogating those who had visited the MLA Hostel that night, in order to compare their narratives with earlier statements and hoping fresh disclosures may tumble out inadvertently. That day an important admission was made by one Manzur Alam. He told the officers something that he hadn't stated earlier.

'Ramzan saheb is an MLA from our area. My house falls

under the jurisdiction of Chakulia police station. Ramzan saheb lives in Kishangunj, he also has a house near my village. I have been to his house seeking help on a case I am fighting with the West Bengal State Electricity Board over a plot of land that is long dragging in court. I have seen Nurul at Ramzan saheb's house quite often, he used to be his personal assistant. His house is in Borodiha village under Chakulia police station area. That's how Nurul had come to be an acquaintance.

'I was in Kolkata on work on December 20th, staying in a friend's rented room in Baker Hostel. I was to meet Sajad Ali, the Karandighi lawmaker, at the MLA Hostel around 10 p.m., regarding a business matter. When I went in, his room (Room number 2/7) was locked.

'I waited for half an hour, but Sajad bhai did not return. So I decided to drop by at Ramzan bhai's room because I knew he was in Kolkata at that time. He would always stay in Room 3/10. I took the stairs to reach his room on the third floor, reached the doorstep and saw the room locked from the inside. There were no lights inside, so I thought he may be asleep. He was not keeping well and I decided not to wake him up at that hour.

'When I turned around and walked towards the lift, I saw Nurul walking towards me from the other end. I asked Nurul, 'What brings you here, bhai? So late in the night?' He told me that he had some work with Ramzan saheb.'

The sleuths were relieved but infuriated. Why hadn't he disclosed this during earlier interrogations? It could have made matters so simple. 'Why didn't you tell us about this earlier?'

'Sir, when I heard the next day that Ramzan bhai had been murdered, I was totally shaken. I was scared! What if I were dragged to court for my statement?'

Meanwhile, the veneer of pretence and innocence was being ripped off at Ramzan's Kishangunj house, as investigators started to unearth every detail about him. They were an influential family, and relatives, neighbours, party members and other associates remained tight-lipped about disclosing information regarding the family. But the job of the police is to achieve the apparently impossible, no matter how tough the means to the end.

The answers to the what-when-why-how came slowly but surely.

Nurul Islam had worked as Ramzan Ali's personal assistant for four years—between 1989 and 1993. Ramzan was taken ill in 1991 when he was detected with diabetes and tuberculosis, and rushed to Delhi for treatment, accompanied by his wife Talat and PA Nurul. He was admitted to Ram Manohar Lohia Hospital, where his treatment continued for quite some time, and this was the time that Nurul and Talat got attracted to each other.

Ramzan was over fifty, frail, and debilitated by severe illnesses. Talat was thirty around that time, and Nurul about the same age. There was no stopping the flames that started to burn inside the two young souls. The inevitable happened. Nurul and Talat were in love, and there was something intense in the relationship.

Ramzan Ali was back in Kishangunj soon, and able to sense the depth of his wife and PA's friendship. The dynamics of their relationship had changed before and after his illness.

One day, he caught the lovers in a compromising position. It led to a bitter conflict. The MLA beat up his PA, sacked him, lashed out at him with unspeakable abuses and threw him out.

Nurul left for Delhi and took up a job with Mumbai Trading & Company. Ramzan was pleased with this development. Finally the cause of the misery in his life had left for another city, and he could have some peace. But the lovers were too smitten to be able to live apart. The physical boundaries had failed to douse the longings of love; if at all, the attraction and ache only increased due to the absence, the craving to be with each other grew so wild that they were willing to take more precarious paths fraught with hazards and uncertainties. Talat and Nurul exchanged regular letters and called each other at least twice every week.

Ramzan would pour his heart out to his brother Hafiz Alam Sairani and some close friends. These were vitriolic rants about Talat and about whether he had misjudged her character. Their relationship is clear from two documents. One, a page from Ramzan's diary obtained from his Kishangunj home. An excerpt:

Today, on 13/4/1992, I am writing this with a heavy heart. Perhaps I did not know the meaning of love. There's no point in hiding that my wife has taken advantage of my illnesses and got involved in a physical relationship in order to fulfil her lust with someone she knows only for a few years. I am being subject to this terrible injustice every day. I was stunned when she told me that she would get married again if she wanted to.

The second document is an un-posted letter written by Talat, to Nurul. The letter, written in Urdu, was found from the same Kishangunj house.

Dear,

Adaab!

Received your letter.

I am going through such torment that I wish to meet you so my troubles may be washed away. People say it right—we get so obsessed in our quest to fulfil our desires we may lose everything else for it. I am scared. Shall I lose you too? My life is nothing but you alone.

~

Nurul hadn't returned to Delhi after the murder. He had fled to Bihar. The police combed and searched every part of Bihar. Another team was in Uttar Dinajpur. After a month of cat and mouse chase, Nurul was finally in the police net on February 27, from Siliguri More of Raigunj.

During interrogation, despite every circumstantial evidence going against him, he did not admit to committing the murder. He stood firm though unable to shield himself against the barrage of questions and arguments.

Renuleena Subba's statement was very important in this case. But she had continued to conform to Talat's original FIR statement. Every time she was asked about the episode, she stuck to her original version, even in court. It was easy to figure she wasn't telling the truth. Obviously she had witnessed the murder and had known the truth all along. But she wanted to protect Talat. Why? We don't know the answer. It is not always possible to know the complete truth.

A quick chargesheet submission, and a lengthy trial followed. Forceful arguments and counter-arguments were witnessed by the court. Talat-Nurul's lawyer claimed that this was a political murder, though the court had no reason to believe it. The string of events was described in court backed up by various circumstantial evidence available in different stages of the probe.

Nurul's handwriting specimen matched with the entry

in Khwaja Habib Hotel's register; the owner of the booth from where Talat used to call Nurul in Delhi had identified her in court; the call list had been procured. In addition, Manzur Alam was an eye witness to Nurul's presence in the MLA Hostel on the night of the murder.

The police also learnt that Talat had often sent Nurul money orders in Delhi from the New Market sub post office. The documents were presented in court in order to indicate the dynamics and depth of Nurul and Talat's relationship. Talat and Nurul had secretly purchased the sub-distributorship rights in a fertiliser company—Jayasree Chemicals & Fertiliser in Uttar Dinajpur. This business deal was an indication of the seriousness of their relationship. Moreover, the pages from Ramzan's diary and Talat's letter that she never posted, were testimony of the disastrous marriage and her new love interest.

The lower court found Talat and Nurul guilty and ordered life imprisonment for both. The Calcutta High Court passed the same verdict. Nurul and Talat are still in prison.

What exactly happened that night? Nurul and Talat never admitted to it, and Renuleena fudged the truth. But the investigating team that spent hours interrogating the three and looked at the case from every possible angle had their own version of the episode that night:

Nurul came down to Kolkata to meet Talat. But meeting outside involved risks, and the lovers wanted to avoid people witnessing their secret meeting. So they decided that Nurul would enter the room once Ramzan slept. Renuleena's presence upset the plan somewhat. Around 10.30 to 10.45 p.m., there was change of sentry duty near the gate. During this time, the security is a bit lax.

Nurul knew it, and had sneaked in, wrapped in a shawl. The person in charge of making entries into the Visitors' Register had also been lax.

Talat had opened the door after 10.45 p.m., when she was convinced that Ramzan and Renuleena were both sound asleep. They were. Nurul entered the room at 11 p.m., and they wanted to spend some time in the area separated from the main room by curtains.

But Ramzan was woken by their soft whisperings. From their muffled voices, he immediately sensed Nurul's presence. Once he knew he had been caught, Nurul was sure he could not escape Ramzan's wrath no matter where he fled. Ramzan was, after all, a powerful man, a politician, who could make his life miserable. Perhaps what happened next was merely in a wild moment between reason and unreason without careful consideration of the ramifications.

In a flash, Nurul pounced on Ramzan and throttled him to death. To make this look like the job of hired killers, Nurul tied up Talat and Renuleena. Then he quietly sneaked out of the main gate, and the sentries never suspected him, knowing that someone who was leaving the premises must have entered legitimately. They were not even supposed to stop and question visitors while they were leaving.

It was no political skirmish that had led to Ramzan Ali's death. But neither was it a planned murder. Neither Talat, nor Nurul were professional killers, and there were thus gaping holes in the narrative scripted by the accused. A surge of emotion and anger had led them to take the decision.

The main objective of investigating a murder is 'to ascertain the truth'. But our truth-seekers do not have the luxury that detective Byomkesh Bakshi had in delving deep into the mindscape of criminals. The inimitable Byomkesh was interested in the criminal's mental landscape and inner vision while unearthing the truth. He wasn't so keen on punishment. When he learnt that a searing compulsion may have coerced a person into committing a crime, he even allowed the criminal to escape the police. He deemed it enough punishment that a person would go through lifelong pain and suffering from their conscience.

But real-life sleuths are humans of flesh and blood who have no luxury to go beyond the paradigm of legal disciplines. A police investigator must remain impassive, nonchalant, he must get hold of the accused, collect evidence, file chargesheets in court seeking punishment. Many offences are committed due to the strange circumstances in which the accused have found themselves. No matter how impersonal and clinical an investigator's approach may be, he often cannot help empathising with the poignant tale of the accused. How difficult is it then to continue with the investigation in a detached way?

Did Mohammed Akram ever feel a tug at his heartstrings during the investigation when the curtains were rising bit by bit and the drama unfolding? Did he view the case as a melancholic drama in which the impossible cravings of Talat had prompted her to such desperation despite twenty years into her marriage and being the mother of three children?

What's the use of such wild speculations! The more you know, the more you know you don't know.

THE ABSENT WOMAN

The Bapi Sen murder case, 2003

Bowbazar police station. Case number 1/2003. Date: 1 January 2003. Indian Penal Code Sections 302, 34, 354: murder, acts done by several persons for furtherance of common intention, assault or criminal force to woman with intent to outrage her modesty.

Mere sapno ki raani kab ayegi tu...chali aa...tu chali aa...

They were singing the old Hindi movie song in chorus. A young man had thrust his head out of the window of a moving taxi and was screaming out these lines in crude invitation to a woman. Others inside the taxi were singing and roaring with laughter.

A woman riding pillion on a two-wheeler was the subject of their drunken invitation. An arm shot out from the taxi window and tried to grab her. 'Happy New Year, daahling!' they yelled.

Somehow she managed to retain her balance on the two-wheeler, clinging onto her male friend, asking him to drive faster. 'This is so scary, so infuriating, let's get out of here, fast!'

But how could one go faster than the taxi that had been on their trail for ten minutes, adjusting its speed and not allowing them out of sight? Not that the road was empty, even if it was past midnight; in fact there were quite a few cars at that hour. But if the biker reduced the speed or increased it, the taxi followed suit so at every moment the taxi was parallel to the bike. There were no policemen around as all of them were possibly on duty in and around Park Street. What now?

Wellington Square and Hind Cinema Hall were up ahead. If they carried on like this, there could be an accident any moment. Confused, bewildered and angry, the biker screeched to a halt, alighted, and took off his helmet. The taxi squealed to a stop too. Five young men alighted, all of them twenty-five to thirty year olds. The woman stood there frozen with fear and anger, their very presence making her want to retch. Her friend asked the five men, 'What are you up to? Please do not misbehave.'

By then, the five men had encircled the woman. When her friend protested, they pushed him aside, 'You can't be having all the fun alone, eh?' One of them held her hand and pulled her towards him, and the others did the same, showering filthy abusive words all the time.

Just as the situation was about to take a turn for the worse, a red Maruti Omni zoomed past, and screeched to a halt fifty metres ahead. Like a scene straight out of a Bollywood chartbuster, a lanky, athletic man alighted from it and made a dash for the spot where the five were harassing the woman.

The tall man strode up to her and enquired, 'What's going on here?' He made a move towards the five louts. 'Leave her. Right. Now'.

'Who are you? Shala! Ah, a pimp! Get the hell out of here. Quick I say.'

It was the night of 31 December 2002 in Kolkata. By

the time the grisly crime was committed, it was well past midnight—on 1 January 2003.

Four days later. January 5, 8 p.m. The Calcutta Medical Research Centre (CMRI) premises were filled with people. A huge contingent from different media houses had filled the place, but the number of police officers and staff far outnumbered them. They had been in the hospital premises for most of the day since the afternoon of January 1, holding on to slender threads of hope.

'Dr Agarwal, please save him. Please! We can't afford to lose him…' the police commissioner pleaded with the renowned neurosurgeon.

'We are trying our best. The neurological status is very poor; he has gone into coma. There are plenty of internal injuries, including multiple fractures of the skull. I really do not know how much I'll succeed in reviving him, but fingers crossed, we are trying our best…' Dr Agarwal signed off despondently.

The Intensive Care Unit (ICU) of CMRI was a flurry of activities. The patient's condition was going beyond control. The doctors were trying their best, but the patient had not regained consciousness since the time of admission. It was as if the final countdown to an inevitable end had begun.

There's no potent, breathtaking suspense of a mystery being unearthed in this case. The accused were arrested within few hours of the crime, yet, the Bapi Sen murder case is among the most talked about in the history of Kolkata Police investigations. It is still a matter of intense speculation as to what exactly happened that night; the sequence of events is still shrouded in mystery even after fifteen years.

It is important to document this case that took the city by storm. Here are the details from the case diary, the drama and arguments of the courtroom, the verdict, and most important, the sequence of events of that night, along with some of the whys and the wherefores.

Narayan Chandra Sen and Renuka Sen, residents of Behala Parnasree, in Kolkata's south-west, had three sons and three daughters. Narayan-babu was a retired Sub-inspector of the West Bengal Police Force. Their eldest son, Joydeb, lived with his family in the quarters provided by his office in south Kolkata's Ballygunge area, the second son, Anup, was an employee of Indian Bank. The youngest was Bapi, who had joined Kolkata Police in 1991 as a sergeant. Their youngest sister Jayashree lived with the parents, while older sisters Mandira and Deepa were married and lived in Maheshtala and Parnasree respectively.

Bapi was married to Soma (in June 1992), and the couple had two sons—Somsuvro, who was six years old at the time of this incident, studying in class one, and the younger one a toddler, just over a year old.

Bapi was the kind of person whom people would generally refer to as a tough guy right from his childhood days. He had seen his father in uniform and had always nurtured a dream to be in the police service too. He was athletic, and had a keen interest in sports—football and table tennis were his favourite games.

In 2002, at the time of the incident, Bapi Sen was posted

with the Tollygunge Traffic Guard. Right from his early days as a young professional, Bapi was known to protest wrongdoing. Once, he had chased and caught a person who snatched a gold chain from a woman on Park Street. Who knew then, that his instinct to always get justice for the wronged would turn out to be the cause of his death when he was just a young man of thirty-five?

31 December 2002

A few introductions are necessary here before describing the incident.

Ashok Sengupta, resident of Netaji Nagar, south Kolkata, bordering the city's fringes. A marine engineer working with a private company headquartered in Mumbai.

Nazibul Hossain Mollah, also a resident of south Kolkata, also marine engineer by profession.

Gautam Majumdar, same profession. Resident of Parnasree, the same area where Bapi lived.

Kanai Kundu, Kolkata Police constable, lived in Behala, the larger area of south-west Kolkata of which Parnasree is a part.

All of them were in their mid-thirties, and had known each other for many years. Bapi was part of this group. They would huddle together for evening addas occasionally on a large football ground by the side of a neighbourhood club. Parnasree Recreation Club was, like several clubs all over the city, a centre for various sports activities, chiefly football and table tennis, occasional carom and cards, and a meeting point of local youth—a typically male dominated home away from home, often a refuge for the neighbourhood men to escape the tedium of family obligations. Here they indulged in their dose of adda, sports, annual functions like theatre, music and so on, with the women's involvement in the club restricted to staging a few functions. No Kolkata neighbourhood is complete without at least one such recreational club.

Bapi was on afternoon shift that day, so after work he went home, changed, had a quick bite and went to the football ground adda spot. Gautam, Ashok, Nazibul and Kanai were already there, engrossed in conversation. Ashok, who stayed in Netaji Nagar about ten kilometres away, told them enthusiastically, 'I got my car along, come, let's all go to Park Street tonight!' And they all agreed.

The red Maruti Omni—WB-02F-4992—headed to Park Street that night, around 9.15 p.m. After they had started off, Bapi suddenly remembered, 'Hey, I had promised a friend from Taratala that I'd visit his place tonight. Can't ditch him. Let's just swing by, and head to Park Street from there.' Taratala was just a couple of kilometres from Parnasree.

The friend was Subrata Basu, whose father was a superintendent in the Merchant Navy trainees' residential training complex. Subrata lived in the government quarters there. His parents were expecting Bapi, but now there were four others along with him. Nevertheless, all were welcomed and urged to have dinner with them. Post dinner, all six young men—Bapi, Gautam, Ashok, Nazibul, Kanai, and now Subrata—set off for Park Street.

The dazzle of Park Street on the last day of the year is special. It's a riot of colours running wild, sparkles of lights everywhere, pulsating blasts of music reverberating around and a turbulent sea of people as far as the eyes can see. The streets had back to back vehicles, as if Park

Street had turned into a confluence of every road from every part of the city.

Ashok parked his car on Russel Street, outside the popular joint Hobby Centre. It was around 12.30 a.m., the friends had all made a few rounds of the Park Street area, taking in its sights and sounds, and now they decided to call it a day.

The vehicles on Park Street were all moving westwards, from Mullickbazar towards Jawaharlal Nehru Road, the Maidan area. There was bumper to bumper traffic, blaring horns, impatient drivers asking those ahead of them to move an inch more. But traffic continued to move at a snail's pace. Bapi, who knew Kolkata roads like the back of his hand, realized it would take a lot of time to reach home if they went with the flow. Better to go against it—take Rafi Ahmed Kidwai Road—first to Wellington, then Ganesh Chandra Avenue, Central Avenue and off to Strand Road. From there, they could go straight to the southern part of the city. That side would have less vehicles and the ride would be smooth.

Ashok took Rafi Ahmed Kidwai Road exactly as Bapi had suggested. Suddenly, as they were approaching Wellington, they caught a glimpse of a taxi running dangerously close to a bike and a pair of hands reaching out from inside the moving cab, trying to touch the woman pillion rider.

Moments later, the speeding bike suddenly screeched to a halt and the biker alighted from it. So did the woman. The taxi too stopped, and five young men came out. There was an argument between the men and the biker for a few moments, then the latter was pushed aside and the men encircled the woman, staggering around her. The woman yelled, trying to push them away.

Bapi, who was on the front seat of the Maruti Omni by Ashok's side (who was driving the car) noticed this from a few metres away. 'Ashok, stop the car ahead,' Bapi told his friend. Ashok did so. Bapi flung open his door and ran out towards the woman. 'What's going on here? Leave her. Right. Now.'

'Who are you? Shala! Ah, a pimp! Get the hell out of here. Quick I say,' came the reply.

Bapi was not bothered by this vulgar, aggressive response. He held one of the men's hands and said menacingly, 'Leave her alone. I am Bapi Sen, I am a sergeant of Tollygunge Traffic Guard.'

'So? We are policemen too! Get the hell out of our way.'

A calamitous fight ensued. Bapi tried his best to fight the five molesters, but they were far more powerful, and used all their strength to rain slaps, punches and kicks on him. Their screams and shouts led Gautam, Ashok, Kanai, Nazibul and Subrata to rush towards Bapi in a desperate attempt to save him. But by then, their friend had already been overpowered, beaten black and blue and thrown flat on the tram tracks. 'Kill him, kill him!' the assailants shrieked while still raining blows on him.

Gautam, Subrata, Kanai tearfully pleaded with them, 'What are you doing? He is a police officer!'

'Really? But is he the only police officer around? Didn't you hear? We too are policemen. Come on, kill this cur.'

Bapi's friends were no match for the monstrous strength of the opponents, and so the kicks, punches went on, on his chest, abdomen, head, even as he was lying inert on the tram tracks, unable to strike back anymore. Blood lay splattered on the road, Bapi's body lay still, it was difficult to ascertain whether he had life in him anymore. Finally, the five attackers, convinced he was dead, or perhaps suddenly aware of what they had done, jumped back into the taxi and fled. Kanai, possibly the most sensible in the group, quickly noted down the number plate: WB-04A-3450.

The bike? Where was the bike, biker and the pillion-rider? When the bitter, gory, street fight was being fought the biker and his friend had quietly left, Bapi's friends now realized when the road suddenly looked eerily deserted. Had those men noticed the biker and his companion fleeing? Was their outrage the result of the catch slipping away?

There was no time to look for the bike at that point. His friends rushed Bapi to Medical College & Hospital. He was admitted to bed number 158 of the hospital's Casualty Block (CB-Top). Around 2 a.m., the doctor on duty said that there was an urgent need for a CT scan. The friends, helpless and worried, ran down the hushed corridors and staircases of the hospital and called Bapi's home.

Rakshakar Mondol, Sub-inspector of Bowbazar police station, was on his usual round of the city. It was one of those unfortunate nights when people all over the city were enjoying themselves, but he had to work at the unearthly hour. Mondol had stepped out of the police station at around 1 a.m. while revellers were still roaming the various lanes and bylanes of Kolkata ushering in the new year. Around 3.30 a.m., he got an anxious call on his mobile phone from the Lalbazar control room: 'Rush to Medical College & Hospital. There's possibly an assault case there.' Rakshakar reached the police outpost just outside the hospital and heard about the incident from Assistant Sub-inspector Brajakishore Chowdhury.

Officer-in-charge of Tollygunge Traffic Guard, Amit Bandopadhyay, who was Bapi's senior at work, also rushed to the hospital along with Bapi's brother Anup.

When the CT scan report came in, a doctor attending to Bapi looked at it carefully, and after a few minutes, eyes lowered, told Bapi's friends and relatives, 'The injury is grievous. You may consider taking him to some other hospital.' The doctor meant that the patient required better medical facilities. Anup, after discussing with friends and family members decided to take his brother to Calcutta Medical Research Institute (CMRI), hoping a sound medical treatment would help him regain consciousness within a couple of days. None of them imagined that the end would come so soon.

Bapi was moved to the Intensive Care Unit of CMRI where he was admitted under the supervision of neurosurgeon Dr Ajay Agarwal. As a new day emerged, the police circle in Kolkata begun to learn about the Rafi Ahmed Kidwai Road episode: a traffic sergeant who had protested eve-teasing was beaten up so badly he was fighting for his life at CMRI; apparently, the attackers were policemen too. The news had spread in no time. Each one of Bapi's colleagues was in shock.

Rakshakar rushed to the Lalbazar Traffic Control Room in the morning. The owner of the taxi with WB-04A-3450 number plate was tracked down from the database immediately: Madhukant Jha. Even the taxi was located shortly, parked on Bipin Bihari Ganguly Street, outside a Kolkata Police mess. Jha was found resting inside his cab.

Madhukant hailed from Bihar's Darbhanga. He had left his native village twenty-four years ago, and had started off as a cook at the police mess in Kolkata. Later, he worked as driver with a Himalaya Opticals showroom. But he wanted to have his own vehicle rather than do the job of a hired driver with a fixed salary. So, in 1996, he took some loans, bought his own taxi, and even appointed Mewalal Gupta, a village acquaintance, as helper. They would both eat at the police mess, having known most of the policemen who lived there for many years.

Who was in your taxi last night? Madhukant named all five without wasting a minute: Madhusudan Chakraborty, Sridam Bauri, Peeyush Goswami alias Gopal, Shekhar Bhushan Gupta alias Bhola, and Sheikh Mujibur Rehman, all constables of the Kolkata Police's Reserve Force. After work, they had gone out for the New Year's Eve revelry in Madhukant's taxi.

Madhusudan and Peeyush were immediately arrested from the mess. Sridam, Mujibur and Shekhar were not there. When the first two were being produced in court, Sub-inspector Mondol found to his surprise that the other three were already there to surrender. They had had a hunch that it would be impossible to get away. The court ordered police custody for all five, but each one denied having committed the crime.

Imagine the police's discomfiture when the news was out in the papers: the protector had turned predator—an officer had been brutally beaten up by his colleagues as he was trying to save a woman from being heckled and teased.

Bapi was lying unconscious in the ICU. The chances of him ever coming back were very thin. He breathed his last on January 6, at six in the morning.

A wave of sorrow hit the Sens' home in Behala. Not just Behala, the entire city mourned Bapi Sen. For Kolkata Police, the only way to make up for this terrible loss—if at all that was possible—was ensuring that the accused got the strictest punishment.

Atanu Bandopadhyay, then Inspector in the homicide

section and now Assistant Commissioner in the detective department, took charge of the probe. Proving the accused guilty was the only option, he knew. Nothing else mattered.

There was, however, a hitch even before the probe began—a major stumbling block at the very outset. Despite a lot of effort, the biker and his female friend could not be tracked down. Her narrative alone would have made a major difference to the probe.

When all efforts came to naught, the Kolkata Police Commissioner issued an appeal in newspapers.

We understand the trauma and suffering you must be going through. Whoever you are, please come forward. Our colleague Bapi Sen was horribly wounded when he tried to protect you from some attackers. He is no more. Your statement is crucial for the punishment of those responsible for his death. We shall be grateful to you for your support, and we will take the responsibility of your safety and security.

But there was no response to the Police Commissioner's appeal.

Atanu Bandopadhyay had long started working on the case. He collected all evidence and submitted the chargesheet on March 10. The trial began.

Lawyers for the accused naturally placed a number of arguments in favour of their clients before the court. Here's a look at the crux of their reasoning, arguments and narrative. They presented a completely different view of the reality of that night. What was their version? What was *their* truth?

They alleged that Bapi had stopped their taxi near Wellington reeking of alcohol and had introduced himself as a traffic sergeant and demanded the blue book and licence from the driver. When the driver refused to give in, Bapi apparently tried to open the rear door so he could jump into the cab. The driver, out of desperation at this sudden interference of a sergeant who was drunk, not in uniform and certainly not on duty, started driving. Unable to get into the moving vehicle, Bapi slipped and fell on the tram tracks. They claimed he had died from this fall. Shockingly, there was no woman, and no eve-teasing in their version.

Driver Madhukant and helper Mewalal, whose statements before the police had matched with Bapi's friends' version, submitted an altogether different narrative when they appeared before the court. At that time, their claim matched with the version of the accused persons: that Bapi was drunk and had fallen on the tracks.

In order to establish Bapi Sen as drunk, the 'Outdoor' ticket of Medical College & Hospital was presented before the court (when Bapi was taken to the hospital first and doctors had attended on him in the hospital's outpatient department). It mentioned primary injuries along with the phrase, 'two pegs of alcohol'. On the basis of this, there was even a discussion in court on Bapi's unrestrained lifestyle.

They claimed that Bapi's friends' identification of the five assaulters in the Test Identification Parade could not be deemed as evidence. Around 1.15 a.m., surely there could not have been enough light on the road to see the faces clearly for them to recall later? They claimed Bapi's friends' arguments were fabricated to frame the innocent constables.

To counter this narrative, the government pleader referred to Atanu Bandopadhyay's probe and the evidence he had collected (on the basis of which the chargesheet had been submitted before the court):

First, the post mortem report. It mentioned the presence of skull wounds and innumerable injuries all over the body. The doctor had mentioned the death as 'ante mortem and homicidal in nature'. It was no accident, but murder.

Pre-empting the questions likely to be raised on the post mortem report, Atanu Bandopadhyay had taken an opinion from Dr Ajoy Gupta, professor and renowned forensic sciences expert, then head of the forensic medicine department, Calcutta Medical College. Dr Gupta said there was 'nothing to suggest primary and secondary impact of vehicle', which meant that Bapi Sen hadn't died on falling from a vehicle. There were certain 'defensive wounds', indicating that it had all begun from scuffles in which he must have tried to defend himself. Countless wounds all over the body suggested that he had been kicked and punched with an attempt to take his life. A wound on the skull was so deep that it couldn't have resulted from a fall on the tram tracks; in fact, his head may have been stamped on repeatedly with something heavy, such as boots.

'Considering the site, size and disposition of injuries on the person of Bapi Sen, it could be concluded that the injuries resulted from fists, blows and kicks by healthy adult individuals with great force that was sufficiently strong to cause fracture of skull with intracranial and intracerebral injuries,' the report read.

Did Bapi drink that night? The outdoor ticket of Medical College & Hospital had the words, 'beaten by fists, blunt injury, two pegs of alcohol', written on it. Who wrote it? Surprisingly, there was no signature on it. Even more surprising—and this did not require medical tests, it was evident to the naked eye—there were two different handwritings on the outdoor ticket, the ink colours distinctly different. How was it possible for anyone to mention a person had taken two pegs of alcohol without a blood test? It was clear that some evidences had been forged and/or tampered with in order to prove that Bapi was in an inebriated state. Dr Agarwal, the neurologist at CMRI Hospital under whose care Bapi Sen was admitted, clearly stated, 'When I examined the patient, who had then just been shifted from Medical College & Hospital, I never thought for once that he had been drinking. I can vouch for this from my years of experience.'

The City and Sessions Court didn't think much of the arguments placed on the basis of the outdoor ticket and the theory that Bapi had slipped on the tram tracks in an inebriated state.

But the court did accept the validity of the Test Identification Parade. Deputy Commissioner of the Detective Department had written to the Calcutta Electric Supply Corporation (CESC) in charge of supplying electricity all over Kolkata inquiring if there was an interruption in the power supply around that time in the area. If the supply was uninterrupted, was it bright enough? CESC's chief engineer informed the police (and also subsequently the court) that there was enough light for anyone to see people and their faces quite clearly.

Two eyewitnesses of the episode that night were tracked down by the police. Ganesh Barik and Samir Ghosh, security personnel of a private company, Jay Matadi Traders, on 38/1 Nirmal Chandra Street, off Rafi Ahmed Kidwai Road were on night duty, and had witnessed the incident.

The judge, on 1 July 2004, in his verdict wrote that this was undoubtedly one of the rarest of cases—unimaginable that members of an organized, disciplined force could so ruthlessly lynch another member of the same force. He admitted to refraining from giving them the death sentence as they were young, and ordered life imprisonment for all five.

The case moved to the Calcutta High Court. The verdict was the same there.

Both judgments praised Atanu's work; in fact, the Kolkata Police Commissioner was requested to officially acknowledge his effort in conducting the probe.

The accused moved the Supreme Court of India. But, looking at the High Court verdict, the apex court downright rejected the appeal for the case's hearing.

Bapi's parents are no more. His wife Soma was offered a job with Kolkata Police right after his death. Now she works in the Arms Act section of Lalbazar, the Kolkata Police headquarters. His older son, Somsuvra is a young man of twenty-one, just out of college, looking for a job. His younger son Shankhasubhro is in class nine.

Bapi Sen's death was front page news in all the leading dailies of West Bengal for months. Why, then, did the woman refuse to come forward, knowing her statement would help grant stronger punishment to those who had killed a young man out to save her? Why did she not respond to the Kolkata Police Commissioner's appeal? Did she not suffer the pangs of guilt?

There is no answer. But shouldn't we look at it from her perspective too?

Of course the woman knew that if she came out in the open, she would have to face police interrogation, the matter would inevitably lead to a courtroom trial. Perhaps she didn't want to expose herself to the tiresome legal scrutiny? After all, people do have inhibitions, scepticism, apprehensions about laws, courts and the police.

Perhaps she knew that the gossip hungry media would have a lurid interest in her personal life. They would subject her to intense scrutiny, and she would find herself in the eye of a storm. Maybe she could foresee her own repugnance at the hunger for television exclusives? Perhaps she did not have the stomach to take this inhuman societal pressure and personal dissection? How many of us can show this kind of bravery to willingly go through it all? Not many can. And you cannot blame an individual without taking into account her reasons for keeping away from ruthless societal and political trials.

Maybe she would have been hailed as extraordinarily courageous if she came forward. But you cannot blame her because she chose not to.

The wounds of Bapi Sen's death are still raw for the Kolkata Police family.

Rabindranath Tagore had written that we must get to grips with reality calmly. But, how is it possible for ordinary souls like us to come to terms with the brutal murder of a helpless colleague who lost his young life trying to save another human being?

THE BILLION DOLLAR NOTE

The Tapan Das murder case, 2003

Bowbazar police station. Case number 49. Date: 7 February 2003. Indian Penal Code Section 302: murder.

'Telephone yes, telegraph yes, telescope yes, teleprinter yes, but telepathy? No, Sir...'

The 'real' Dr Hazra, after an attempt on his life, bruises all over, swollen face in gauze dressing, had gone to a police station in Rajasthan to look for the abducted child Mukul, seeking Inspector Tiwari's help.

This scene, from the film *Sonar Kella*, written and directed by Satyajit Ray, had these hilarious lines delivered by Inspector Tiwari. And it comes to mind here because of a parallel in a curious case investigated by the Kolkata Police a few years ago.

When Dr Hazra from the film said he was a parapsychologist, the inspector was both amused and baffled. No, he had never heard of such a thing. Dr Hazra gave it another shot and asked him if he knew of the word telepathy, to which the inspector responded with the above lines. Inspector Tiwari's lines are still popular and oft-repeated by Ray fans.

Now, if we apply these lines to our story here, it may sound almost as baffling: billion dollar question yes, billion dollar smile yes, billion dollar deal yes, but billion dollar note?

Obviously the answer would be a firm and resounding 'No, Sir!' That's how sleuths in our homicide department reacted when they heard about the existence of a billion dollar note while handling a case under the Bowbazar police station's jurisdiction, almost fifteen years ago. It even earned the sobriquet 'The Billion Dollar Case' during trial.

Walk towards Central Avenue from Esplanade (Dharmatala in people's preferred lexicon), and there will be Jadunath De Road to your right. A typical central and north Kolkata lane, incandescent and sophisticated without being flashy, reflecting the elegance of a bygone era. A few paces into Jadunath De Road, there's Hotel Penguin that is quite well known in this part of the city. In fact, St Joseph's College and Hotel Penguin are landmarks if one looks up Jadunath De Road on Google maps.

~

7 February 2003

The phone at Bowbazar police station rang a bit late in the morning: 'Sir, calling from Hotel Penguin. There's been a murder, Sir. Please come down urgently!' a breathless, hysterical voice informed. It took officers not more than five minutes to reach the hotel from the police station. The detective department had been informed, and officers from the homicide section rushed there from their Lalbazar office that was not too far away either.

What was the matter? Room number 102 was a double bedded room on the hotel's first floor: the hotel's register showed that Suman Bihari and Motilal Shaw had checked into the hotel on February 6. Motilal had left around evening and no one had spotted him returning till late into the night. The following morning, housekeeping staff went about their routine work cleaning every room. Only the boarders of room number 102 refused to open the door despite repeated ringing of the bell. The housekeeping staff waited patiently for half an hour. It was possible that the boarders were sleeping in.

After half an hour, the knocks turned into frantic loud blows. Still no response. Suspicion and worry gripped the senior hotel staff, and eventually the manager decided to open the door with his set of duplicate keys.

The scene inside the room was spine-chilling. Suman Bihari's body lay on the bed, face down. It wouldn't require an expert to figure out that there was no life left in it anymore. Blood had oozed from the nose and mouth and the blotches had turned hard and cold. He was in a white shirt, cream coloured half-sleeved woollens and grey trousers. There were no other marks of injury visible on the body. Possibly, he had been strangulated.

An empty beer bottle was lying in one corner of the room, along with a twelve-page edition of the *Sangbad Pratidin* newspaper of February 6, with one page missing.

A place where a criminal act occurs is known as the place of occurrence, or PO in police parlance. A PO is the first step in a long and winding stairway, which, if examined with intelligence, patience and diligence, may have the keys to help open the door to the mystery lying at the end of the long climb.

Sleuths leave out nothing during the examination of the PO. The beer bottle was carefully examined—no sign of clear hand or fingerprints that could be 'developed' were found. These were collected because one couldn't take a chance with these things. A newspaper of February 6 *Sangbad Pratidin* was quickly procured from the daily's office and the missing page was read carefully. There was nothing on that page or the ones found from the room that gave the sleuths any important clue.

Bedcover, pillows, mattress, corners around dustbins, bed, chairs, tables, mirror, ceiling fan, AC machine, even the basin, commode, and cistern in the bathroom—every inch of the room was subjected to an intense combing operation but, alas, nothing was found that could show them the next step ahead.

Only a tiny notebook with some names, addresses and telephone numbers was found from the trouser pocket of the murdered person. In the absence of other clues, the sleuths were elated with this find.

Names, addresses and phone numbers from the notebook led the police to identify the dead person. He was not Suman Bihari as the hotel's registration book had showed. The deceased was Tapan Das who stayed as a paying guest in a house on Raicharan Pal Lane of east Kolkata's Topsia area. The person whose paying guest he was had been identified as Purna Chandra Saha, a middle-aged man who promptly recognized the deceased.

Saha told the police that Tapan was a quiet, withdrawn man who hardly spoke. Apparently, Tapan told him he ran a business, but gave no indication of what it was. Yes, some guests visited him occasionally, but no, he certainly wasn't married. Only a brother of Tapan Das could be tracked down—a resident of Khardah in North 24 Parganas, close to Kolkata's northern fringes, who wasn't too perturbed about the news, and told the police in all frankness that he hadn't been in touch with Tapan Das for many years.

The post mortem report arrived, and quite predictably, indicated that it had been death by asphyxiation. The body was cremated.

'Murder in City Hotel, Assailant Flees, Police in the Dark'—headlines of this nature filled all the dailies, questioning the safety and security of the people living in the city. It led to an obvious pressure on the police force, especially on the detective department, demanding a quick resolution. Go bring the murderer whoever he is and wherever he is hiding and get him quick!

Get him for sure. But who? And from where? Sleuths wracked their brains, but they were still engulfed in a silence and darkness that can only come from complete cluelessness.

Every staff working at the hotel from the morning of February 6 till the door was opened with the duplicate key had been interrogated. What did the murdered person's companion look like? Funnily enough, the description of the hotel staff couldn't even help detectives draw a stick figure, it was so vague.

He was of medium height, slightly dark, a bit on the heavy side. How could that come of any use? At least five hundred persons fitting that description could be found in a one kilometre radius of the hotel. Spectacles? No. Bald? No. Anything significant that you can recall that made him stand apart? Any mark on the face? Did he hobble or walk unsteadily, with a limp? No, Sir, can't recall any such thing. Did he have any unusual style of speaking? Didn't notice, Sir, only that he was speaking in Hindi while writing his name in the register, but the words had a hint of Bengali in the pronunciation.

From this information the sleuths deduced that the murderer, now on the run, who had entered his name as 'Motilal' in the hotel register, was also a Bengali. It was already clear that the deceased was a Bengali too.

But more important was to find out the reason they had checked into the hotel under aliases instead of their real names. Why were they trying to pass off as Hindi-speaking people? What was the criminal intent or devious plan behind these carefully taken steps? Where was the answer to untangling these knots?

The sleuths resorted to the only clue they had at their disposal—the notebook containing sundry phone numbers and addresses. Most were numbers of people based in North 24 Parganas district, located in Kolkata's north. One call led to another, one person led to the other till they safely concluded that that the deceased Tapan Das was a confirmed cheat and that was his job and source of sustenance. He would cheat young men and women with job promises, con people by assuring he would get banks to sanction loans quickly.

They also stumbled upon something incredible—Tapan Das had recently come in contact with a unique gang of swindlers. Around that time, the rice pulling trick was a scam which was creating a stir among the villagers of North 24 Parganas district. This was reported in the media too. What exactly is 'rice pulling'? A sensational claim was doing the rounds that some old metal utensils had acquired the property of pulling enormous quantities of rice towards them as if these had turned into veritable magnets. There were rumours that the price of metals that had acquired this unique power was skyrocketing in the international market. Every other household had people bringing together utensils and rice, waiting to see if they got pulled towards each other. Greed and ignorance had sucked them into this incredible trap.

Some scammers decided to make the best of the

situation—surely they could con some people to make a quick buck? They went around introducing themselves as agents of metal sellers, promising they would get the metals of utensils tested against some advance payment. Many got cheated in this manner. Not just in West Bengal, the same rice pulling trick had created a sensation all over the country at different times.

Those investigating the Tapan Das murder case got hold of some gangs involved in the rice pulling trick, and interrogated them about the murder. No one had a clue. Only, they admitted to having seen a man of average height, dark, slightly heavy, but nothing beyond that. No address or name was found. The investigation did not progress even an inch.

What now? A good investigator must have one essential quality—to never get bogged down by failure.

Back to the hotel. Another round of marathon interrogation of the employees for hours on end. A policeman needs immeasurable patience and cleverness to frame the same question in various ways. For, you never know which question may trigger a memory reminding people of something they hadn't said before. The same line is rehashed, reiterated: 'Come on, think hard, can you recall something?'

Finally, a possible clue—somewhat fragile and amorphous—appeared in sight. A room service man told interrogators that on February 6, he had delivered a plate of chicken pakoda and salad to room number 102. This was known to them already from the hotel bills. After the first order, came the second order for a second plate of chicken pakoda. That too was known. Hotel bills of course! So what was *his* input? He said that when he was leaving the room after serving the second order, the two boarders were having an argument.

What were they arguing about? As far as he could remember, he had heard the word 'circus' a number of times.

Circus? Was this, then, the much awaited clue? Were the two boarders associated with a circus? Had they watched a circus the day before? Or cheated a circus employee?

Circuses are no longer popular. But they used to be at the time of this incident when circuses had their own set of audiences in cities, more so in villages. The murder took place in February, a whiff of winter was still around, and circus companies would not have wound up their tents still. With the word 'circus' picked up from the conversation, the next focus area for the Lalbazar sleuths was circus companies in the city and suburbs.

Sketches of the murderer drawn from the descriptions of the hotel staff were shown to employees of the circus companies. Could they recognize this man? A lot of hard work went into going and asking people around, but the result was zero—there was no pointer, no indication, not a single clue.

What now? Surely this was another dead end, was the thought running through the minds of the despondent team of investigators as they returned from a circus company's office in Naihati of North 24 Parganas district. The trip and the questioning had served no purpose. This was one of those cases that would remain unresolved, they thought. But then, when nothing goes right, there may be a stroke of serendipity and fortune smiles down on you once more. The breakthrough came en route to Kolkata.

The car was speeding towards Jagaddal, leaving Naihati

behind moving through Ghoshpara Road. The tired officers decided to take a quick break for tea somewhere convenient up ahead. The driver, a resident of Noapara, an area not far from there, told them, 'Sir, there's Circus More ahead, should I stop the car there? There's a good roadside tea stall I know of.' The car stopped at Jagaddal's Circus More.

Sipping the steaming cup of tea, one of the officers had a brainwave, as if a shock of electric waves had run through him. He told the others, 'What if the room service boy hadn't heard the entire conversation? Maybe only the word "circus" remained as a residue in his memory from "Circus More"? The murderer was in touch with the swindlers of North 24 Parganas district. Can't circus mean Circus More?'

The others agreed that this was quite possible. The hotel employee never meant to eavesdrop, and it was perfectly possible that he could remember only this word. Why not check out this Circus More area?

Sources—all the pundits and talents in the criminal world—dived into the gullies and mohallas of Jagaddal's underbelly. In a couple of days, they were ready with information about a man who matched with the description of the person seen at Hotel Penguin. The Motilal in the hotel register was a disreputable character named Bapi Mukherjee! He was held by the police.

There is a perception that a few slaps are a prerequisite for confession before the police. But Bapi Mukherjee blurted out everything, perhaps the sights and silences of the interrogation room at Lalbazar were enough to make him utter the phrase that's music to the ears of every interrogator: 'Don't hit me, Sir. I'll tell you everything!'

The murdered and the murderer were both expert cons. They had met at Jagaddal railway station and the two hit it off like a house on fire.

Tapan Das had managed to lay his hands on a fake billion dollar note from one of his friends. Many tricksters trying to sell fake million and billion dollar notes had been arrested at that time in various parts of India and abroad. Bapi was slobbering at the prospect of getting some of these notes himself, and he had no idea whatsoever that the notes were all fake and didn't exist in reality.

Tapan, a trickster of the first order, whose many machinations included getting a kick out of fooling other talented fraudsters like himself, knew that Bapi was associated with the rice pulling gangs. Tapan chalked out a plan and he told Bapi that he was a major player in this field and was in contact with agents dealing with precious metals used for rice pulling. It was such a roaring business that he had acquired billion dollar notes through it. He could introduce Bapi to the agents if he gave him some advance money.

If Tapan was out and out evil, Bapi knew how to give him a taste of his own medicine. He handed over some money to Tapan to buy his trust initially. Tapan took him to Kolkata, promising to introduce him to some agents. Possibly he had planned to introduce him to some people who would pose as agents and get Bapi to pay him some more. Bapi on the other hand, had devised another plan—he wanted to steal Tapan's billion dollar note at night after he slept. Two tricksters with two different plans had come together and rented a room to cheat each other, both registering themselves under false names.

There was an argument on the afternoon of February

6 while drinking beer. Tapan demanded more money to introduce Bapi to the agents. An angry Bapi wanted the advance back, and said he suspected it was a hoax. He didn't want to sell the precious metals nor did he wish to be a billionaire. Better to get the money back. The argument led to a scuffle, and Bapi wanted to snatch the billion dollar notes from Tapan. The two were scrimmaging through the room, and a desperate Bapi held Tapan's throat in a tight grip.

He held on to his throat until the life seeped out of him. Even after he ensured Tapan had died, Bapi waited for a few hours in the room. Then he picked up the billion dollar note and quietly slipped away after sundown, locking the door from outside. He took out a page from the *Sangbad Pratidin* newspaper and put the door key in it (this key was later retrieved from his Jagaddal home).

What happened to the billion dollar note? Bapi tried to sell it a number of times, but it didn't take him long to figure out that the piece of paper was of no value whatsoever. Eventually, bitterly frustrated, he tore it up.

The murder mystery was solved. But what about punishment? A Sub-inspector in the homicide section, Subhashis Bhattacharya headed the investigation. Now he is Inspector in the anti-cheating section of the detective department.

It needed to be proved through forensic tests that the pages of *Sangbad Pratidin* containing the hotel key in Bapi Mukherjee's Jagaddal home and the remaining ones in the hotel where Tapan Das was found murdered, was part of the same 16-page edition newspaper. This was done.

A handwriting sample of the accused and that of the hotel register matched through scientific tests.

It also needed to be proved that the key found in Bapi's home was the key to room number 102 of Hotel Penguin. There was no way the accused could escape from the chargesheet containing all the evidence now.

The court ordered life imprisonment for the accused and he is still in prison today.

The investigators had the last laugh. Or maybe they just quietly smiled their billion dollar smiles?

HER TRUSTED MURDERER

The Ravinder Kaur Luthra murder case, 2007

Ballygunge police station. Case number 17. Date: 15 February 2007. Indian Penal Code Sections 302, 394: murder and voluntarily causing hurt in committing robbery.

It looked like a typical after-party scene in a plush house.

Expensive brands of whisky, rum, vodka, wine and brandy were stacked in the liquor cabinet in the drawing room. None of these bottles would be within the reach of the average drinker. Cushions were strewn around the couch, three plates with forks were placed on a stylish, glass centre table. One of the plates had two pieces of chicken reshmi kebab in it, another had a half-eaten paneer pakoda, and remnants of salad, bits and pieces of raw onion rings, tomatoes and cucumbers lay on the third plate. There were some paper napkins stained and crushed after fingers had been wiped on them, as well as two glasses with a few sips of a golden liquid, possibly whisky, left in them.

Three colourful candles were burning in the room—not your run-of-the-mill, ordinary candles available in neighbourhood stores, but expensive ones that were nearly the size of cricket wickets and took several hours to burn.

In one of the three enormous bedrooms in the flat a woman lay sprawled on the floor, her body covered with a large comforter that went right up to her chest. It was clear that there was no life left in her.

She was remarkably athletic and strong for a fifty-one year old, probably the result of regular exercising. But all of that had not been enough to save her life, though there were clear signs that she had put up a fierce fight—a few strands of hair were caught in the grip of her right fist. The murderer's hair, no doubt.

A deep strangulation mark was visible around the throat, along with a deep gash from something sharp, like a hook. Her nail ends had something dark under them—another indication of the painful tussle. Clearly, she did all that was humanly possible to fight the assaulter. There were deep wounds around her eyes, on her face, neck and throat.

It was a cold, calculated murder. Who could have killed her so ruthlessly? Was it one person? Or, were there many hands in the murder?

~

The packets of milk were lying on the ground, just outside the door. On all other days, there's a basket kept there to drop the milk packets in. Three newspapers, *The Times of India*, *Anandabazar Patrika* and *The Economic Times* were also lying on the floor. The milkman and the newspaper vendor had rung the bell several times, but left soon afterwards. They had work at hand, and there was no time to waste. Everyday, Nikku, who had worked in this flat for several years had opened the door just after one ring.

The vegetable vendor was there, too. He was waiting outside as the Ballygunge Bhabi ordered fresh vegetables over phone every week, which a worker from Maiti Vegetables of Jadubabu'r Bajar went to deliver. Two others were waiting—the maid Radha and the driver Ayub. It was nine in the morning, and it was unusual that no one had answered the door yet. Even if memsahib was sleeping till late, at least Nikku should have opened the door by now. What was he up to?

Ashok Poddar from the opposite flat came out, worried. Asit Mohan Luthra, owner of this flat, had left for Vizag on work two days earlier. He had spoken with his wife the previous evening, too. But her mobile and landline phones had both been ringing since morning, and no one was taking the calls. A worried Mr Luthra had called his neighbour Ashok Poddar, 'Could you please find out if everything is all right?'

At 9.15 a.m., Asit Luthra spoke with driver Ayub from Ashok Poddar's phone.

'Are the cars in the garage?'

'Haan saab.'

There were two cars, a Toyota Corolla and a Honda City. In fact, Ayub had rung the bell about half an hour ago, but when no one had opened the door, he had gone to check the cars wondering if memsahib had left in one of the cars on some urgent work.

The information further worried Mr Luthra.

'Ayub, rush to Parveen madam's house, find out if she is there.'

'Jee saab.'

Sudesh and Parveen Talwar, both fifty year olds, lived on Dover Road. Sudesh owned a leather export business and his wife Parveen ran a gym in the house. The Luthras and the Talwars were close friends and spent time at each other's place quite often. Asit Mohan Luthra's wife Ravinder Kaur Luthra was in Parveen's gym for workouts thrice a week.

But no, she wasn't at the Talwars' home. Sudesh and Parveen rushed to the Luthras along with Ayub. By the time they arrived, the caretaker of the building complex and security personnel were standing outside the door along with other residents—curiosity, fear and worry gripped them. It was impossible for anyone to break into the main door. There was an automatic lock on the door.

The building was Tripura Enclave, 59 Ballygunge Circular Road. It was a housing complex guarded by lofty walls in a plush Kolkata neighbourhood with Ballygunge Science College to the east, St. Lawrence High School and the Ballygunge Military Camp to the west.

It was a ground floor plus seven storeys building. The Luthras lived on the seventh floor. A high wall separated the terrace in two parts and the west side was owned by the Luthras. It was impossible for anyone to climb onto their part of the terrace.

One would need to take the staircase from inside the Luthras' flat to enter their terrace. The winding stairway went up from their drawing room. A gate separated this space into two parts, but it remained locked from the Luthras' side. The door to the Luthras' side of the terrace—connected through the staircase from within their flat—had, by its side, the keys to the terrace gate lock. Only if someone had taken the keys of the locked gate that connected the two sides from the Luthras' side, would they be able to open it and only then would someone be able to enter their personal terrace.

The Luthras' terrace was lush green. There was a servants' quarter in one corner where Nikku lived, with an adjoining room with glass walls for their two dogs Fandy and Beagles, who spent the night there. The rest of the terrace was a manicured lawn with soft greenery and foliage, a flower garden and an artificial fountain flowing down a mound of pebbles and rocks, its gurgling sounds gentle and calming.

The housing complex had three gates—one for the entry of cars and people, another for exit, and the third, an emergency gate that remained shut most of the time. There were two blocks in the complex—'A' and 'B', both eight floors high. The ground floor was used as parking space. 'A' block had three flats on each floor—Unit I, II and III. 'B' block had one flat on the first floor, and the remaining floors had two flats each. Taken together, there were thirty-four flats in the complex. The Luthras lived in B block.

The residents had ensured tight security arrangements for the complex. Mac Security Service, a private agency, had a supervisor and three security persons each managing security at the gate and reception desks of the two blocks in three different shifts.

Each block had two lifts and two staircases. One lift was meant for emergencies, and therefore remained locked, and was without a liftman. The residents themselves operated this lift when required. Reception areas had close circuit television cameras with video linkage to every flat. The security men at the desk had to send photographs of visitors to the flats concerned, and alert residents through the intercom. Only after getting a green signal from the resident the visitors could enter using either the staircase or the lift. Domestic workers and regular visitors like friends and relatives known to the security men due to their frequent visits were kept outside this stern vigilance.

No one could enter the locked flat other than by using a ladder to get into the Luthras' side of the terrace. Someone got a ladder and Ayub used it to jump onto the other side;

the keys were kept exactly where they were supposed to be—by the side of the door used to enter the Luthras' flat. Ayub opened the gate and the others entered. There was no trace of Nikku. Where *was* he?

The pet dogs were inside the glass room. Their anguished, desperate barks and scratching on the door could be heard from outside. They had never had to stay in the terrace room for so long as they roamed around in the flat through the day, and so their horror and despair was understandable.

Once inside the flat, the Luthras's friends and neighbours found signs of a party concluded a few hours ago, and then Ravinder Kaur Luthra's body on the bedroom floor.

One of them moved the comforter. Mrs Luthra was in a blue floral printed night dress and socks. Other than the deep wound of strangulation mark on her neck, there were no other signs of assault on her.

The cupboard and drawers were in complete disarray. It was later learnt that the diamond ring on Mrs Luthra's finger was gone. So was a huge amount of jewellery from the cupboard and drawers, and rupees three and a half lakh in cash kept in a leather bag, and nearly four hundred US dollars. In a nutshell, all the valuables from the flat had gone missing.

Those who had entered the scene of crime were stunned into silence. 'We need to inform the police immediately,' the first to stutter these words was Ashok Poddar, his mind a horrified muddle. Sudesh Talwar nodded, 'Just a minute…I have the Lalbazar Control Room saved on my phone.' Parveen had the number of the Ballygunge police station too, so she began to search for the number in her mobile phone contact list.

First, a call was made to the Ballygunge police station, and then another to the Lalbazar Control Room at 10.15 in the morning.

'There's been a murder! Please come down quickly! Is the OC there?'

~

Fifty-four-year-old Asit Luthra owned a security agency—GI Securities with branches all over India, even abroad. It was a thriving business. Asit and Ravinder were the picture of a perfectly happy couple. Their older son Kabir, twenty-five-years old, looked after his father's business in south India. The younger, Angad, had just turned twenty and was studying in London. Mr Luthra travelled frequently on work. In fact, he had gone to Vizag on a business trip on February 13, and was scheduled to return on February 21. He rushed back by the afternoon flight on February 15, following the news of his wife's brutal murder.

Nikku Jadav, the person supposed to be in the flat, but who in fact couldn't be found anywhere around was a young man of twenty-five who hailed from Bihar's Banka district. Nikku had been working as the Luthras' domestic worker for seven years. He had joined work as a teenager, when he was just sixteen years old. He cooked, made necessary purchases for the household including all odds and ends, and ran errands all day.

Ayub had been employed with the Luthras for even longer. He was sixty years old, and had been their driver for thirteen years. Mita and Saraswati were full-time maids. Both had gone on leave since February 11 and a temporary worker, Radha, had been hired for a week to fill in for them.

A teary-eyed Radha told the neighbours that Mrs Luthra had released her from work last night at 8.30 p.m., asking her to report early the next day. By the way, while leaving, Radha had seen a gentleman in the drawing room. Nikku of course, was there too, she thought it pertinent to inform.

A gentleman? Who could it be?

Pradip Lal. Around fifty years old, he ran a successful tin container manufacturing business. He lived close by on Rowland Road. Pradip and his wife Sunila were known to the Luthras socially for many years. Last evening, Pradip Lal had dropped by to meet Asit, but after learning that he was out of town, Asit had chatted with Mrs Luthra for an hour and a half.

He rushed to Tripura Enclave by 10.30 a.m. on hearing the news of the murder. Yes, he was there last evening, Mr Lal himself told the neighbours.

But Nikku? Where was he? Had he vanished into thin air?

~

Officers from the Ballygunge police station reached Tripura Enclave, followed by sleuths from Lalbazar's homicide section; the latter had been informed by an urgent call from the Lalbazar Control Room.

But how were they to step inside Tripura Enclave? A rabble of angry residents had gathered outside the complex. Some residents from the adjoining multi-storeyed building complex, Saptaparni, had also heard the news and joined them. Policemen were lambasted with some lines the officers were now quite familiar with: 'What's the point of your coming here now? Our worst fears have come true. How can an assailant sneak in and murder someone? No one ever notices police patrol vans in this area. Today such a thing has taken place on the seventh floor, tomorrow it will be the fourth floor, day after, it'll be the third floor...'

Policemen are accustomed to this kind of angry outburst. They pleaded with the assemblage, and asked them to be allowed inside the flat. Additional force was sent from Lalbazar to quell the agitation.

Inside the flat, several fingerprints were found in the rooms—the cupboard, glass, couch, bedroom mirror and drawers were full of them. The Police Commissioner asked the homicide section to conduct the probe and Sub-inspector Ashique Ahmed was to lead the investigation.

The incident was bound to create ripples and it did. Soon rows of journalists' cars were parked outside Tripura Enclave, including a couple of Outdoor Broadcasting vans. 'Breaking News' flashed on television screens. 'Brutal murder in multi-storeyed building, police in the dark', or 'Lalbazar's role under question over city's security'. There were all kinds of opinions and views on this.

The homicide department, however, wasn't perturbed by these criticisms. It wouldn't be tough to crack this one. Ashique could clearly see the newspaper headlines tomorrow or day after: 'Murder mystery cracked within 24 hours, servant arrested'.

The closure was just a matter of time as it was an open and shut case. Nikku had committed the murder and fled with the valuables. It was a murder for gain. But where would he flee and for how long?

Mobile phones had come to India twelve years before this incident. Nearly everyone carried mobile phones, including Nikku. The police had his number and even if it were switched off, his call details and last location could be obtained, all within a maximum of forty-eight hours. The technical surveillance had started already. He had no earthly means to get away.

This complacency was punctured by just one phone call that came on the Luthras' landline phone while the police were preparing a sketch of the bedroom.

'I am calling from Shambhu Nath Pandit Hospital. A young man of around twenty years of age was admitted here by the traffic police a little while ago. It was a road accident, there's head injury. We got this number from his ID card in his wallet, there's a picture on it too. His name is Nikku Jadav. Is he a family member? We are transferring the patient to SSKM Hospital, his condition is unstable.'

What was *that*? Nikku had met with an accident? Was there a larger conspiracy and had someone attempted to wipe out Nikku?

A police team rushed to SSKM Hospital. Nikku was not in a state to talk to them as he was unconscious. There were dark patches of dried blood in the corners of his eyes. A doctor said that he had fallen head first onto the footpath from a bicycle. He had suffered trauma to the head and also had gashes all over the face. He needed an urgent CT scan and had to be brought back to consciousness. If his condition turned critical, he would be referred to the neurology department.

One of the officers in the investigating team told the doctor, 'We need to talk to him as soon as he regains consciousness. It's somewhat urgent. I think you may have heard that there was a brutal murder in Ballygunge. This boy used to work there and his statement is vital.'

The doctor gave the officer a dirty look. Then said as politely as possible, 'I think for the time being we ought to figure out how to save his life. Let him regain consciousness, talk to him then…I mean, if at all he regains consciousness, that is!'

Nikku's accident jolted the officers out of their complacency that the case would be solved quickly. The cops ruminated on possible theories for the murder, raised questions, and decided on the possible direction the investigation ought to take.

One, the CCTV footage must be looked into thoroughly especially to find out who had gone in and come out of the Luthras's block in the past twenty-four hours.

There was a problem here. The CCTV at the reception had been installed in such a position that only those who were unfamiliar and would have gone to the area where security men sat would be visible on the camera. In case a person was familiar and did not need to go through the checks, they could quietly take the lift beyond the CCTV camera's range. This was a major flaw that could make a huge difference.

Asit Luthra ran a security agency. How could he have missed out on this? Still the video footage needed to be looked into for all it was worth.

Two, names of all security personnel and domestic workers for both blocks of the complex needed to be compiled. Did anyone have a history in crime? Did the Luthras have any enemy? Did Asit Luthra have a business rival?

Three, the residents, too, were within the circle of suspicion. Mrs Luthra and many others residents lived affluent lives—swanky cars, gym, tennis, golf, clubs, kitty parties were part of their routine. Could there be a murderer among them because of some internal jealousy or rivalry?

And then, the date of the murder—February 14, Valentine's Day. Now everyone seems to celebrate it, but eleven years ago, only some affluent homes celebrated Valentine's Day.

There was a party at the Luthras that night. Who was there (or who *were* there?) on Valentine's Day evening in Mr Luthra's absence? How long did they party? Were they from other flats in the complex or had they dropped in from outside? There were two glasses on the table. Was there only one person apart from Mrs Luthra? Who was it?

Four, the mobile numbers of all security people and domestic workers had been listed, so their call details and tower location could be checked. Not a single person could be left out of this scrutiny. It was important to find out the exact details of each person's whereabouts at the time of the murder. Their fingerprints would be taken and checked with those found inside the Luthras' flat.

Five, Mita and Saraswati, the full-time maids, had to be summoned. What made them go on leave at the same time? Radha was working for a few days only. It was possible, and there were plenty of incidents to back up this theory, that some people took up jobs as maids in affluent homes in order to find out everything about the family and meticulously plan a robbery.

Six, and very important, Nikku's accident. Had Nikku been the murderer, as it had been suspected earlier, he would have fled. When a traffic constable found him lying on the footpath near Jadubabu'r Bajar, he did not have any bag with him. If Nikku had all the money and jewellery, surely he needed to put them into something? According to the security guard, Nikku had left the building at 5.45 a.m. with a huge jute bag. So where was the bag? Did

Nikku see something that required him to be bumped off? Would an eyewitness have been risky for the assailant?

Had Nikku staged the accident? He could not be taken off from the suspected persons' list, though he was undergoing treatment. Someone known to Mrs Luthra was definitely involved in the conspiracy even if more than one person was involved. It was certainly possible that Nikku had opened the door to the murderer in the dead of the night.

Seven, had one or many persons entered the flat? Mrs Luthra was quite strong. It wouldn't have been easy for one person to overpower her. Perhaps Nikku was not alone and had an accomplice. The accomplice may have tried to eliminate him to avoid sharing the loot or did not want to be blackmailed. Perhaps looting was not the real reason—the theft just a way of diverting attention from the real reason behind the killing?

Eight, was there any underlying tension in Mr and Mrs Luthra's relationship? This was important too. Pradip Lal's role was questionable too. He had talked about dropping by to meet his friend, Asit, but had stayed on and chatted with Mrs Luthra for an hour and a half even after hearing that Asit wasn't home. At a time when mobile phones were used by all for sharing every bit of information, was it acceptable that Pradip did not know about Asit being out of town? All right, even if we buy that logic, how long could a person talk to a friend's wife? Wasn't an hour and a half a bit too long?

The investigators were now pretty bewildered by the weight of all the doubts and the barrage of questions they were asking themselves. What did they know? What did they not know yet? Ashique was preparing these lists in his notebook. He had thought this would be a smooth ride, but no, it didn't look all that easy. The officer-in-charge of the homicide section put his hand on Ashique's shoulder and asked, 'What's all this brooding about?'

Ashique looked up at his boss, 'Sir, it looks a bit complicated.'

The flow of incidents, the twists and turns would have made any real-life investigator distraught, even the famous sleuth who lived on 21 Rajani Sen Road, would certainly have ruminated and said, 'It's a bit bewildering for sure, Topshe'.

~

The sleuths of Kolkata Police stoically waited at the SSKM Hospital. Nikku regained consciousness around afternoon. Thankfully, the CT scan report showed that his head injury was external, there had been no internal haemorrhage, and he could be released within a few hours.

'Doctor, we need to know something from him. May we speak with him?'

'Today? Do you really need to? The patient is still in trauma.'

'If it's possible…'

'All right, do ensure you don't stress him out too much…'

The same dirty look from the doctor. This time, the police ignored it. The doctor would do his job, the police, theirs.

Lalbazar, meanwhile, had started following up on the other loose ends. The tower location and call detail records for nearly fifty odd mobile phone numbers were being tabulated by the technical wing. Maid Radha, driver Ayub, some security personnel from Tripura Apartments, the vegetable-seller from Jadubabu'r Bajar Madan Maiti, had all been taken to Lalbazar for questioning. The Talwars, Ashok Poddar, and Pradip Lal would come in any moment. Another list for the next interviewees was being prepared. One or several persons were either lying or suppressing the truth, that was clear. Now the questioning should find out the exact loopholes.

Ayub wept bitterly. A local source had informed the police that he had had a showdown with the Luthras recently over salary hike demands. When he was pressed, Ayub whimpered, 'Memsahib loved me a lot. I can never commit such a sin, Sir.'

When Nikku was brought to Lalbazar, he was staggering, gasping for breath, tired and terribly ill. He was sore with pain and struggling to talk. The officers were in a dilemma, should they question him at all? Somehow he tottered into the room and drank some water offered to him.

But what he narrated blew the officers away—they had not been prepared for another dramatic twist in the tale.

'Mr Lal left around 9 p.m. last night. Radha had left before him at 8.30 p.m. Around 11 p.m., memsahib opened the door to a woman and a man. The lady was wearing jeans and top, and the gentleman was in kurta-pajama. I can't recall having seen them earlier.

'Memsahib was a good cook. She had taught me to cook all kinds of dishes—Chinese, Continental, Mughlai… After dinner last night, she asked me to stay back in the kitchen because the guests were expected.

'After the two guests dropped in, she asked me to prepare kebabs and pakoda. I did as instructed, and also prepared a plate of salad. Memsahib and the gentleman were drinking. The lady asked only for water. I prepared and served all this on a tray with an ice-box. There were often such late-night parties in the flat and I had to stay awake till late. Last night's party went on almost till dawn. I had dozed off in the kitchen.

'Suddenly, my sleep was broken by the noise of people shouting. I don't remember the time. It could be two-thirty or three in the morning. Memsahib and the lady were having a bitter argument, while the gentleman was trying the pacify them. The woman walked out angrily. The gentleman stayed on. I couldn't sleep after that.

'Memsahib had asked me to leave early and get flowers for puja and some medicines, so I left at around five-thirty or quarter to six on a bicycle.'

'Was the gentleman still there?'

'Yes, memsahib and he were in the bedroom. The door was shut.'

'And then…?'

'When I was heading towards Jadubabu'r Bajar to buy flowers, out of the blue a bike came, hit me and sped away. My head hit a lamp pole, and I nosedived onto the footpath. I don't remember anything after that.'

The sleuths were in a terrible dilemma. Nikku's statement matched with that of the security personnel on the timing of his departure. He had seen Nikku leaving with a jute bag. Had the murder taken place after Nikku left? Or before that, inside the locked bedroom? Who was the woman who had stomped off around 2.30 to 3 in the morning? Who was the man in kurta-pajama?

'Can you identify the man? What about the woman?'

'Most certainly, Sir. One glimpse and I'll identify both of them.'

Artists from the homicide section were sent for urgently.

They started working on the 'portrait parle' based on Nikku's description of the two late night visitors to Mrs Luthra's flat. The sleuths decided to show the portraits to residents of Tripura Enclave.

It had been a long day. There had been marathon interrogations and inquiries. At around 11.30 p.m., the officers investigating the case decided to call it a day. By the next morning, some specific pattern in the movement of residents would be evident from the technical wing's analysis of their phone call lists. Mita and Saraswati had been summoned already and they would arrive too; the other residents would be interrogated.

Ashique found it vexing that there had been no clear direction so far. He was trying to fit the different parts of the jigsaw puzzle of this extraordinary crime. The CCTV footage showed no signs of the lady and the gentleman who were now chief suspects. The position of the CCTV allowed for easy entry into the building if someone familiar chose to carefully slip away from the camera's sharp, prying eyes. Were they guests of some other residents? Possible. There were Valentine's Day parties in many flats and many unfamiliar faces inside the building complex. Perhaps they were among them?

It was 11.45 p.m. when the Talwars, Ashok Poddar and Pradip Lal left Lalbazar in their respective cars after long interrogation sessions. A car was called from the transport section to drop Radha, Ayub and Nikku home. Ashique reminded all three that they must be present at Tripura Enclave by ten the next morning. There were more questions to be asked, more answers required.

As Nikku was about to step into the car, Ashique felt a wave of pity for the young man, so tired and forlorn, and he put his hand on his shoulder and told him, 'Don't forget to take your medicines!'

Nikku nodded, but at the same time, his body involuntarily twitched from this slight touch and he uttered an agonised 'uff'.

Ashique moved away his hand in reflex. 'What's the matter?'

'There's a wound, Sir. Never mind.'

Saying this, Nikku tried to get into the car, when Ashique stopped him. His heart was racing, he had sniffed something.

'Just hold on for a minute... Where is this wound?'

'Near the neck.'

Ashique's senses, dulled by hunger, thirst, fatigue, suddenly came back to life.

'Let's see what wound it is...'

'It's an old wound, Sir...'

'Leave that to me. Open your shirt first.'

Nikku was suddenly loath to opening his shirt. Ashique looked at him. The face that had winced with pain now showed signs of anxiety.

Nikku was taken back to the interrogation room where he had to open his shirt, and a deep scratch could be seen on his neck. It looked like lacerations made with nails. The doctors had naturally been busy treating his head injury and had either not noticed it, or ignored it.

'How did you get this wound?'

'The fall, Sir... the bike came and hit me in the morning... the accident caused this wound...'

'So then why did you say a little while ago that it was an old wound? Moreover, you fell on your face, how did you get a wound on your neck?'

Beads of perspiration had begun to form on Nikku's forehead. One of Ashique's colleagues held Nikku by the neck, and asked menacingly, the roar of his voice taking the young man's breath away, 'Tell us what happened? Sir, he will blurt out everything, he just needs a few blows. Shall I go ahead?'

Ashique intervened. 'Aah! He has a head injury… Let him be… he will tell us everything anyway.'

Sometimes a sugarcoated pill is all that is required to extract the truth. Once caught on the wrong foot, it is only a matter of time before even a seasoned, intrepid criminal breaks down. Nikku was a mere novice. Now he started to narrate what had happened last night to a group of astonished sleuths.

'I had been planning this for a while, Sir. The salary was barely enough for a hand-to-mouth situation. After sending money home, I was hardly left with anything for myself. I used to think, would I spend all my life working as a servant? If sahib was home, I couldn't have done it, so I waited for him to be away, as he frequently went out of town on work. I was looking for the right opportunity.'

'But why did you have to kill? Couldn't you just steal the things and run away?'

'Where could I have run away, Sir? You would have hounded me out, even if I were in my village. Sahib had my photograph and address. I wanted to buy some land and do farming. So I planned something which would bring the money yet I wouldn't be caught.'

'Hmm.'

'Last night, Mr Lal dropped in, and left at around 8.45 p.m. Radha had already left for the day by then. I went off to sleep after dinner. Memsahib also went to bed after dinner. I put Fandy and Beagles inside the glass room at 11.30 p.m., though I kept their leash with me.'

'Go on…'

'Around 1 a.m., I came out of my quarter and entered the flat, and knocked on memsahib's bedroom door. After some time, she responded with a faint, "who is it?" I said "This is Nikku. I am feeling terribly ill, I've got a splitting headache, could you give me a medicine?" She opened the door right away, and I pounced on her. She was taken unawares, and completely startled initially. I pushed her to the floor and wound the dog leash around her throat. But she was a regular at the gym and very fit. She used her finger nails and made a deep wound on my neck and back, then used her fist—she wore a diamond ring—to punch me in the eye.'

'The blood clotted on your eye is the wound from her punch?'

'Yes, Sir!'

'Come on, go on…'

'But she couldn't keep at it for very long after that. Her breathing stopped after some time. Then I took the keys, opened the cupboard, took the money and jewellery and put them all inside a leather bag that had been kept in the drawer. It was Valentine's Day or something… a day of ishq-mohabbat, love. Many flats had been decorated with balloons. Parties were often organized at our flat, too… so I decided to prepare the scene of a party in the drawing room.

'Memsahib was lying dead in the bedroom, yet I went into the kitchen and started cooking. I prepared chicken kebab and paneer pakoda. I took out a bottle from the cabinet and poured a bit of it in two glasses. There were candles in the kitchen, and I lit up those too. I took napkins, spoon, fork and kept them on the table in such a way that would make it appear like there was a late-night party in the flat. No one entered the flat after Radha had left. I had made up the whole story.'

'You left at 5.45 a.m.?'

'Yes, because the security guard would have been suspicious if I left earlier. It was quite chilly, so I took a muffler and wound it around my head so no one would notice the scratches along my neck. I left the building and called Bablu from an STD booth.'

'Bablu who?'

'Bablu Mondol. His home is in the same village as mine, in Bihar. He lives in Ananta Apartment in Alipore. He is a cook in Narenda Baglia sahib's house. I wrapped the leather bag containing money and jewellery in a paper and kept it in Bablu's care. He was keeping unwell for sometime, I didn't tell him anything about the contents. I said I'm leaving it here, I will come and collect it later. He is a simpleton and he believed me right away. I disposed of the jute bag on the way.'

'Bablu has the leather bag?'

'Yes, Sir.'

'We'll go there right away. But first, tell us the story of the accident.'

'As I approached Jadubabu'r Bajar, I deliberately rammed my bicycle onto the street lamp post. I knew it would hurt, I knew I might fall unconscious. In fact, I desperately wanted to be unconscious for a couple of days. I didn't know I'd be discharged so quickly.'

'What if the injury was severe and you died?'

'I had to risk that, Sir! If I ran away, everyone would have suspected me...'

After this long narrative, Nikku took a deep breath, almost relieved it was all over for him. Ashique called the Deputy Commissioner, detective department, on his mobile phone.

'Sir, case cracked. Nikku has confessed. He staged the entire party scene.'

The detective department chief headed towards Lalbazar right away. When he met Nikku, Ashique introduced him with a twinkle in his eyes, 'What a great actor, Sir. Just listen to the story. He does deserve a Filmfare award, if not an Oscar.'

The next part of the story went along the expected lines. The police stormed into Bablu's quarters in Ananta Apartment that night and the leather bag was there. All the money and jewellery was retrieved. Nikku had kept the dog leash—the murder weapon—underneath the mound of rocks and pebbles of the decorative terrace fountain. Forensic experts said the additional wound on Mrs Luthra's neck was possibly a cut from the leash hook. There were several fingerprints all over the room that matched perfectly with Nikku's.

There were no eyewitnesses in the murder. But circumstantial evidence was irrefutable and conclusive and the Alipore District and Sessions Court ordered the death sentence for Nikku. The case moved to the Calcutta High Court. The verdict was life imprisonment.

When someone reposes faith in someone, they do so after walking together on the same path for a while, and then the trust becomes unconditional. That is exactly the kind of trust Mrs Luthra had in Nikku. She doted on him, her trust in him was beyond question. She would leave money and jewellery unlocked in the cupboard, with full faith in Nikku.

She could never imagine in her wildest dreams that the value of that trust would be her own life.

www.ingramcontent.com/pod-product-compliance
Lightning Source LLC
Chambersburg PA
CBHW070308240426
43663CB00039BA/2485
* 9 7 8 9 3 8 7 6 9 3 0 0 5 *